A CHAIN OF LOVE

A Chain of Love

Mother Teresa
and her Suffering Disciples

Kathryn Spink

First published in Great Britain 1984
SPCK
Holy Trinity Church
Marylebone Road
London NW1 4DU

British Library Cataloguing in Publication Data

Spink, Kathryn
    A chain of love.
    1. Teresa, *Mother*   2. Decker, Jacqueline de
    3. Nuns – India – Calcutta – Biography
    4. Missionaries – Belgium – Biography
    I. Title
    266'.2'0924   BX4705.T4455

    ISBN 0–281–04099–0

Typeset by Inforum Ltd, Portsmouth
Printed in Great Britain by the Anchor Press, Tiptree

Contents

How happy I am to have you all; often when the work is very hard I think of each one of you, and tell God: look at my suffering children and for their love bless this work and it works immediately. So you see you are our treasure house, the power house of the Missionaries of Charity.

Some of the beautiful letters of the Sick Co workers we should publish - it will helps many people to love Jesus more.

lc Teresa mc
5/4/83

1

MOTHER TERESA
'I need souls to pray and suffer'

> I need souls to pray and suffer for the work.
>
> MOTHER TERESA

In 1948 a solitary nun left behind her the relative security of the Loreto school in Calcutta and stepped out into the city's streets to live as one with the poorest of the poor and to found a new Congregation committed to their service. Today Mother Teresa's mission, which began so unpretentiously in some of India's most disease-ridden slums, is a universal one. The founding of the Missionary Sisters of Charity was only the beginning of a development which was to include a similar Order for men, contemplative branches of the two Congregations, spiritual links with over four hundred enclosed Orders and an association of some 800,000 lay helpers, or Co-workers, scattered throughout the world. Mother Teresa herself has become the reluctant holder of a string of honours, including that most acclaimed of all accolades, the Nobel Peace Prize, which she accepted 'unworthily' but 'gratefully in the name of the poor, the hungry, the sick and the lonely'. The 'success' she insists is not hers. She is only 'the little pencil in God's hand', and the secret of such achievement is faith in the 'joyous insecurity of Divine Providence', prayer – the solution to every insoluble problem, and the constant awareness that she is but a channel for God's particular love for the suffering poor of this world.

Mother Teresa's work as a Missionary of Charity began as a direct response to the poverty and suffering of Calcutta. From her window in the Loreto convent school she could see the slums of Motijhil and when, finally, she was able to walk amongst the people who lived there, she saw in them the suffering Christ. The city's abandoned children were the infant Christ seeking another Nazareth, the sick who lay down to die in the gutters were Christ re-enacting his passion in the world. The starving destitutes were the people with whom Christ in St Matthew's Gospel (Matt. 25.40–43) specifically said that he identified – they were Christ homeless, Christ naked or imprisoned, Christ hungry and thirsty.

Inscribed in every chapel of the Missionaries of Charity throughout the world are the two simple words, 'I thirst'. The aim of Mother Teresa's Congregation is to 'quench the thirst of Jesus Christ on the cross', the thirst which is the physical, symbolic expression of a spiritual cry for acceptance and love. It is to this end that the lives of the Sisters and Brothers are totally dedicated. Indeed, much of what they do would be impossible without the conviction that they are responding to the needs of the Christ present in man. Money, for example, could not enable them to see beauty in open sores and experience joy in circumstances which rationally should engender despair. Someone once remarked somewhat rashly to Mother Teresa that he would not touch a leper for a thousand pounds. 'Neither would I', was the instant reply, 'but I would willingly tend him for the love of God.' The special quality of love, joy and compassion which Mother Teresa and those who work with her bring even to the most humble or abhorrent of tasks can spring only from their belief that in tending to the broken bodies of the least of their brethren, they are literally touching their Lord. At the centre of their every action lies the mysterious certainty that those who suffer have a very special relationship with Christ; and this relationship is of a dual nature, for if God has identified himself with those who suffer, it follows that those who are so close to him as to share in Christ's passion have a unique spiritual potency. In the work to satiate the thirst of the crucified Christ, the sick, Mother Teresa insists, can do most.

Recognizing that hope and unlimited compassion alone were not enough to meet the needs of Calcutta's poor, Mother Teresa went to Patna for a short course in nursing and dispensary work before starting life in the slums. It was in the chapel at Patna that she was joined quite unexpectedly by a Belgian woman, dressed as she was, in a simple cotton sari. Jacqueline de Decker's calling, it transpired, was remarkably similar to her own. Both women had experienced a vocation to give their lives to God while still in their teens. In Mother Teresa's case, at the age of twelve she had already been convinced of her calling to the religious life. This was later reinforced by fervent and inspiring letters written by a Jesuit priest working amongst the destitute in the Archdiocese of Calcutta. Accordingly, at the age of eighteen she sought admission into the Congregation of Loreto nuns who worked in Bengal and, after completing her novitiate in Darjeeling, taught history and geography to the children of relatively privileged Calcutta families. However, on 10 September 1946, a date now celebrated annually as 'Inspiration Day', came what Mother Teresa describes as 'the call within a call'. In a train taking her to a hill station in the Himalayas she heard what she identified as a second call from God. She had already been called to the religious life and to her there was never any question of abandoning it, but the second call was to another form of service within that life. She was to leave the convent and help the poor whilst living among them.

Jacqueline de Decker's calling to India was shaped by a similar desire to serve the poor and by the conviction that God needed human hands to reach those who most needed him. Her first impulse was to join the Missionary Sisters of Mary who also worked in India, but a brief stay in their convent in Belgium convinced her that her vocation was to serve God in the world as a lay person. Jacqueline was a graduate of the great Catholic University of Louvain, where she specialized in sociology. She also obtained a Diploma in Nursing and First Aid and together with a group of like-minded lay people she made plans to use these skills in Madras. The war, however, postponed any arrangements for sailing to India. When Antwerp was severely stricken and deserted by the vast majority of its doctors, Jacqueline de Decker gave invaluable medical assistance to the wounded and displayed such courage in helping the Resistance movement that she was later to be decorated for her services. At the conclusion of the war, however, with the advice and assistance of a Jesuit priest, Jacqueline finally left for India.

While Mother Teresa was still awaiting permission to leave the Loreto Order, Jacqueline had already begun her work amongst the poorest of the poor. Sadly, the Jesuit priest who had urged her to do medical social work in Madras died unexpectedly on 31 December 1946, the very day of Jacqueline's departure from Belgium. Consequently, when she arrived in India she found herself with little financial or even moral support. Nevertheless, living alone and on a pittance, she won the recognition and the affection of the Indians with whom she worked. Her very poverty attracted their admiration, for the local people were quick to appreciate that living alone amongst the poor as one of them was a very different matter from living in a European community to undertake social work. Jacqueline adopted the Indian way of dressing and eating. She took her food sitting on the floor and slept on the ground. She also made it clear that she was prepared to help anyone in need, no matter whether he or she was Hindu, Muslim, Protestant or Catholic.

The parallels between Jacqueline's life of commitment and Mother Teresa's own conviction that was to lead to the founding of an Order, whose members would dress in the cheapest of saris and eat the simplest of diets and whose concern would be not to convert people to Christianity but rather to make a Hindu a better Hindu, a Muslim a better Muslim, etc., are immediately apparent. There are many other similarities. Like Mother Teresa, Jacqueline speaks of an 'inspiration day' on which she received a second call from God. There is even the suggestion that the calls heard by both women were identical in their wording, but for both such experiences are hidden treasures, about which they are reluctant to speak. 'You remember in the Gospel', confides Mother Teresa, 'what the man did when he found the hidden treasure – he hid it.' Jacqueline de Decker's own account will provide far more profound insights into the nature and purposes of the link between the two women. Suffice it here to say that in Patna they discovered that, in Jacqueline's words, 'they shared the same ideal'.

Jacqueline de Decker's intention was to join Mother Teresa's new Order but her time in India had already revealed serious health problems. At the age of fifteen she had had a diving accident. Doctors had failed to identify the extent of the injury incurred at the time but the heat and discomfort of India had aggravated the problem and caused her considerable pain. It was, therefore, decided that she should first return to Antwerp for medical treatment. In Belgium it was discovered that she was suffering from a severe disease of the spine, further complicated by her body's tendency to produce abnormal fibres. Massaging a sick friend one day she noticed the beginnings of paralysis in her arms. One of her eyes became paralysed and so too did her right leg. The reason why her right shoes were constantly worn out made itself all too strikingly apparent. Eventually she was informed that in order to avoid total paralysis she would have to undergo a number of operations. Grafts were put in her neck and two other places. She spent an entire year in plaster and then in the space of one month she had twelve further grafts to her vertebrae.

Gradually it became apparent that Jacqueline would never be able to return to India and that her total commitment to India's poor and diseased and to what she had so profoundly believed to be God's will for her, was not to be. The realization was initially a bitter one, fraught with a sense of personal failure, but it taught complete surrender to the rationally incomprehensible will of God, and it also demonstrated more eloquently than any words that from every experience, however apparently negative, something positive and constructive may spring.

In the autumn of 1952 Jacqueline received a letter from Mother Teresa:

Today I am going to propose something to you. You have been longing to be a missionary. Why not become spiritually bound to our society which you love so dearly. While we work in the slums you share in the merit, the prayers and the work, with your suffering and prayers. The work here is tremendous and needs workers, it is true, but I need souls like yours to pray and suffer for the work – you'll be in body in Belgium but in soul in India where there are souls longing for our Lord, but for want of someone to pay the debt for them, they cannot move towards him. You'll be a true Missionary of Charity if you pay the debt while the Sisters – your Sisters – help them to come to God in body.

I need many people who suffer who would join us as I want to have (1) a glorious society in heaven, (2) the suffering society on earth – the spiritual children and (3) the militant society, the Sisters on the battlefield. You can be in body in your country but a missionary in India, in the world. You must be happy, as you are chosen by the Lord who loves you so much that he gives you a part in his suffering. Be brave and cheerful and offer much that we may bring many souls to God. Once you come in touch with souls, the thirst grows daily.

For Jacqueline this letter brought the realization that she was not being rejected by God but being granted instead a special role. Her task was to offer joyfully a life of suffering and pain for the work of Mother Teresa, and she accepted it all the more readily because Mother Teresa's proposition was the reiteration of an earlier experience in which she had felt herself to be asked by God whether she was prepared to suffer for him. Without hesitation she undertook to become spiritually bound to the small congregation in Calcutta, but the Missionaries of Charity were beginning to grow in number and as they did so, Mother Teresa's vision of the Sick and Suffering as lives which would form 'a burning light consumed for souls' grew accordingly.

In January 1953 she drafted the basis for the 'Link for Sick and Suffering Co-Workers':

I am very happy that you are willing to join the suffering members of the Missionaries of Charity – you see what I mean – you and the others who will join will share in all our prayers, works and whatever we do for souls, and you do the same for us with your prayers and sufferings. You see the aim of our society is to satiate the thirst of Jesus on the cross for love of souls by working for the salvation and sanctification of the poor in the slums. Who could do this better than you and the others who suffer like you? Your suffering and prayers will be the chalice in which we the working members will pour the love of souls we gather round. Therefore you are just as important and necessary for the fulfilment of our aim. To satiate this thirst we must have a chalice and you and the others – men, women, children – old and young – poor and rich – are all welcome to make the chalice. In reality you can do much more while on your bed of pain than I running on my feet but you and I together can do all things in him who strengthens us.

There will be no vows unless some get permission from their confessor to do so. We could get a few prayers we say, for you to say them also, so as to increase the family spirit, but one thing we must have in common – the spirit of our Society: total surrender to God, loving trust and perfect cheerfulness. By this you will be known as a Missionary of Charity. Everyone and anyone who wishes to become a Missionary of Charity, a carrier of God's love, is welcome but I want specially the paralysed, the crippled, the incurables to join for I know they will bring to the feet of Jesus many souls. In our turn the Sisters will each one have a Sister who prays, suffers, thinks, unites to her and so on – a second self. You see, my dear sister, our work is a most difficult one. If you are with us, praying and suffering for us and the work, we

9

shall be able to do great things for love of him – because of you.

Personally I feel very happy and a new strength has come in my soul at the thought of you and others joining the Society spiritually. Now with you and others doing the work with us, what would we not do? What can't we do for him?

Mother Teresa herself was linked not only to Jacqueline but also to two people in India: one a young girl called Agnes who was dying of tuberculosis in Patna but who 'talked only of souls'; the other a boy named Nicholas who was crippled for life and unable to move. Nicholas lived on the brink of starvation for his parents were very poor. 'And yet', wrote Mother Teresa to Jacqueline, 'the only time he weeps bitterly is when I do not visit him for a long time.' It was on the strength of the prayers and offerings of these three that Mother Teresa survived what, by her own admission, were some of the most arduous times of her life, at first alone and then with only a handful of Sisters in the Calcutta streets. 'Our Lord must have a good laugh', she confided, 'when I attack him with the sacrifices of the three of you for souls. That is how I have been conquering his heart lately, so you see what power you have with God now as Missionaries of Charity.' Convinced that it was due to the intercession of those who were willing to give their broken bodies to repair the sufferings of the world that God was blessing her work, she urged Jacqueline to find others prepared to offer their pains for her increasing number of Sisters.

Recovering from what was only one of the thirty-four operations that she had undergone to date, Jacqueline de Decker sought amongst her fellow-patients and sufferers for those who would be prepared to pray for an adopted sister, to write to her once or twice a year and, above all, to accept from the heart the mystery of suffering offered in faith and love for the work of a virtual stranger in a far distant land. This acceptance represented a special challenge to faith; yet to Mother Teresa it was a beautiful vocation. In a letter dated October 1954 she wrote:

> What a beautiful vocation is yours – a Missionary of Charity – a corner of God's love – we carry in our body and soul the love of an infinite thirsty God – and we – you and I and all the dear Sisters and the Sick and Suffering will satiate that burning thirst – you with your untold suffering, we with hard labour, but are we not all the same one – 'as your Father in me and I in you', said Jesus.

Remarkably, there were many who were able to respond to this vocation and accept the challenge of loving God 'not for what he gives but for what he takes'. In the same year, despite the poverty and the rigorous discipline of the Order, there were already forty-eight Missionary Sisters of Charity. There were also forty-eight Sick and Suffering links ready to share in the spirit of the society and to offer their pains for a 'second self'.

There are in the world today approximately 3,000 Sick and Suffering Co-workers. Over the years Mother Teresa's message to Jacqueline and to all the other suffering links has remained the same but it has become no less fervent:

> We the Missionaries of Charity, [she reminds them] how grateful we must be – you to suffer and we to work. We finish in each other what is wanting in Christ. What a beautiful vocation is ours to be the carriers of Christ's love in the slums – your life of sacrifice is the chalice or rather our vows are the chalice and your sufferings and our work are the wine – the spotless host. We stand together holding the same chalice and so with the adoring angels satiate his burning thirst for souls.
>
> My very dear children let us love Jesus with our whole heart and soul. Let us bring him many souls. Keep smiling. Smile at Jesus in your suffering – for to be a real Missionary of Charity you must be a cheerful victim.
>
> There is nothing special for you to do [claims Mother

Teresa] but to allow Jesus to live his life in you by accepting whatever he gives and by giving whatever he takes with a big smile.

From over thirty-one nations including several iron curtain countries the sick have offered themselves for this task and often from the opposite corner of the world the Missionary Sisters and Brothers of Charity respond. A letter from one Sister Superior illustrates what a spiritual link of this kind can mean to those whose role is to work amongst the destitute and the poor:

I am so grateful to God, that he has given you to be my link as a Sick and Suffering Co-worker. What a privilege it is to have someone praying for me and offering all their pain and suffering for the work that God has called me to do. When I experience tremendous strength and comfort whilst dealing with difficult problems, and when I see how I have been able to manage and cope even when it seemed impossible, I know that my link is praying for me and suffering in her own body so that my pain and suffering may be less. Only in heaven will we be able to judge the power of prayer and the strength it gives to carry on doing God's work, even amidst difficulties. So please, keep on offering your pains and suffering as I have to deal with so many people, sisters, new houses, etc., in order that Christ's love may be given to all. Every day you are also in my prayers so that the Lord will give you all the grace and strength you need to accept cheerfully all the pain and suffering the Lord sends you so abundantly. He *will* give you his grace to bear it. He knows to whom he can send these sufferings. He reserves them for his favoured and close friends so that he can draw closer to them and make them bear fruits of holiness.

The system is not perfect. The rapidity with which the Sisters and Brothers can be moved from one country to the next inevitably gives rise to problems in locating them. For this reason and because of unreliable postage systems or confusion over names the letters which to some represent an invaluable part of the relationship can go astray. Misunderstandings can and do arise. Sick and Suffering Co-workers may not at first fully appreciate that the link must remain an essentially spiritual one – personal gifts and donations to individual Sisters are not permitted. They may feel discouraged by the infrequency of replies from Missionaries of Charity who are allowed to write to them only twice a year and who sometimes do not even fulfil this small quota. For their part, the Sisters and Brothers, caught up in the immediacy of the need which surrounds them, may not always appreciate how much even the briefest of letters would mean to their Sick and Suffering link. Yet, remarkably, these difficulties are for the most part overcome. The national co-ordinators struggle nobly to keep in touch with their Sick and Suffering; and surrounded by bulging files and mountains of correspondence, in her flat in Antwerp Jacqueline de Decker compiles innumerable letters, each one written by hand because the use of a typewriter causes a pain which is now intolerable. In this way she remains impressively up to date with the movements of the Missionaries of Charity, and frequently herself keeps in touch with those whose pains she can in the fullest sense appreciate. She and others are also able to provide a solution to language difficulties by making translations where necessary.

Where there is a need on the part of the Sick and Suffering Co-workers, ideally healthy Co-workers are ready and available to meet it. Where the Sick and Suffering are disheartened, they are offered reassurance and hope. Those who are despondent at the absence of response from their link are gently reminded that it is they who are the spiritually mature links in the chain, and not the young Sister or Brother who may well be unready as yet to appreciate fully the nature and importance of such a relationship.

'Pope John XXIII, speaking on suffering, stressed the need to find a purpose in it. In the love of Christ there is no life

13

without suffering. So', writes one of the Brothers, 'we cannot escape it and we must do all we can to help one another find a purpose in it. If we can find a purpose for accepting his cross as Jesus Christ accepted his own then one will never feel alone.'

At its most fundamental the link for Sick and Suffering Co-workers has achieved this end. Three thousand suffering people have been given a sense of purpose and the Sisters and Brothers to whom they are linked have found new strength and companionship in the knowledge that someone is praying specifically for them. In this way the suffering have themselves brought energy to those who go out to alleviate the suffering of the world, and the value of this achievement alone cannot be overstated. Yet over and above this, those who suffer in the belief that they are sharing in Christ's passion very often become living witnesses to Mother Teresa's repeated assertion that holiness is not the privilege of the few. To a world in which suffering represents one of the principal barriers to belief, they provide a living demonstration that suffering can and does draw people closer to God.

Many of the Sick and Suffering are reluctant to speak about themselves or of any particular spiritual insight or experience other than the Eucharist. Many have a very simple love and faith and nearly all proclaim their own unworthiness in the conviction that they have nothing to offer. Nevertheless, it is the aim of this book to let those who suffer speak for themselves for there can be none better qualified to provide an insight into suffering than those who have actually experienced it, frequently to an agonizing degree. Mother Teresa often speaks of her 'hidden, unknown saints'. Holiness is not a question of great intellect or stature but rather of the kind of understanding that springs from the heart, of faith quietly accepted and of complete simplicity. In response to a comment about his extraordinary patience, one man who had lost a leg in two operations and whose limb was still showing no sign of healing, replied quite simply, 'I have to be'. In this brief but poignant answer may lie the key to much. The Sick and Suffering Co-workers are subject to all the usual human frailties and emotions. One speaks with understandable irritation of all the 'holy hens' fussing round her wheelchair and instructing her to 'offer up her pains'. Another tells how, when confronted in a crisis with the statement, 'How Jesus loves you', he cannot help the reaction, 'He's got a funny way of showing it'. Yet another cites a story of St Teresa of Avila as an example of her own feelings on suffering: 'St Teresa, when on an unusually difficult journey, complained to God of the obstacles he was placing in her path. When he seemed to reply, "But that is how I treat my friends", the saint answered sharply, "Yes, Lord, and that is why you have so few of them!" '

Many of the Sick and Suffering have experienced the desire to commit suicide. Some are deeply introspective; others are resolutely practical and even humorous. One English lady, whose psychopathic husband had killed both her baby and himself, provided the unforgettable comment: 'Well, my dear, all life's a rugger scrum. Someone's bound to get hurt!' 'And', she added, 'when people say, "Why me?", I say, "Why not you?" '

The Sick and Suffering come from all age groups and all walks of life. They also belong to a wide variety of denominations and creeds. So it is that the letters and the accounts that follow include, among others, those of Roman Catholics, Protestants, Hindus and Buddhists. In his book *Autobiography of a Yogi*, the Hindu Yogi, Paramhansa Yogananda, describes an encounter with Thérèse Neumann, the Roman Catholic stigmatist, in which both set out to test the authenticity of the other's spiritual calling and both came to the recognition of a meeting point at the highest, hidden, non-rational level of belief. It is in this spirit, it may be suggested, that the letters of the sick should be approached. God reveals himself to each according to the receptivity of the individual and man interprets the truth from the limitations and diversity of his own experience and perception.

Often it is simply a question of vocabulary. Mother Teresa's vocabulary is very much that of Roman Catholicism, but her message is also one of supreme tolerance: 'God has his own ways to work in the hearts of men and we do not know how close they are to him, but by their actions we will always know whether they are at his disposal or not.' Thus if the individual chooses what may be called the 'Christian way' of living – and of dying, whether he is Catholic, Protestant, Hindu or Muslim he will draw nearer to God.

It is possible to discern in the letters of the Sick and Suffering a multitude of issues over which controversy might arise: undue concentration on what might be termed the 'pre-resurrection Christ', experiences of ecstasy, vision and voices which might be seen as psychic and operating at the level of emotional consciousness, rather than at the level of true spirituality, the efficacy and value of shrines and holy places . . . The list is potentially a very long one, as indeed is the series of criticisms which might be levelled at the writers. Levels of self-deception, the unconscious or even the conscious choice of suffering, susceptibility to auto-suggestion, spiritual pride, the hardness that can arise from constant struggle – they are all there for those who seek to find them. Yet what matters is not this human fallibility but the fact that like the Grotto at Lourdes or a Buddhist mantra, all these people can point beyond themselves to a reality that is infinitely greater. God is at work through his imperfect instruments, insists Mother Teresa, and the more ordinary the instruments the greater the glory due to God. Remarkably, she is not alone in this understanding, for if there is a single, common prayer which emerges, though sometimes only silently or from between the lines of the letters of the Sick and Suffering, it is, 'Assimilate and use the shortcomings and the shadows of my life!' Perhaps this is the very basis for Mother Teresa's assertion that the sick can be especially effective in a work that infinitely surpasses human capabilities but which mysteriously depends on human fidelity and generosity of spirit. Stripped, and weak to the point of being unable even to pray, many are possessed of that most easily lost of all virtues, humility, a genuine belief that they are useless dependents on God alone. So it is that they reiterate, with a very special sincerity, the words of St Paul, 'Not I, but Christ who lives in me'.

Fundamental to any understanding of the Link for Sick and Suffering Co-workers is an appreciation of the fact that it does not mean a desperate craving after healing but rather the constructive use of suffering. Acceptance is of prime importance and in this respect the Link has a very distinctive role, for while medical and scientific progress has transformed the picture in many illnesses and healing in many forms continues to take place, the sum total of illness and suffering seems to remain the same. The objective of healing and wholeness seems to draw no nearer and suffering, it would seem, is an inescapable part of the human lot. To Mother Teresa it is certainly an essential part of the Christian way. 'The following of Christ is inseparable from the cross of Calvary. Without our suffering, our work would just be social work, very good and helpful, but it would not be the work of Jesus Christ.' 'Suffering is not of God,' she acknowledges. A sense of healing mission was central to Christ's understanding of himself and of the work that his disciples were to perform, but God can be at work in the delays, no less than in the moment of release from sickness.

Those who suffer with faith, no matter how imperfect, seem frequently to make an extraordinary discovery: that they are part of one body, the body which not only died on Calvary nearly two thousand years ago, but which dies daily in the children of God and which daily rises again. Paradoxically, in this mysterious, irrational discovery which begins with an acceptance of suffering, lies healing and resurrection. It is a healing which manifests itself not at the level of the physical but rather in the intangible part of man and its mark is the unique joy that springs from having come face to face with a universal and enduring reality.

So very many of the Sick and Suffering display a courage

which far exceeds mere endurance and an extraordinary capacity to communicate happiness if only with an all-embracing smile or the brief touch of a warm hand. To the healthy, suffering borne and transcended in this way proffers, like the wounds shown to Thomas, the invitation to reach out, to touch and to believe. Thus once again the healing process is at work, for suffering can be the medicine that deepens our humanity. In the direct encounter with those who suffer there is much not simply to be given but also to be received if only we approach humbly in the knowledge that we, in our own way, are as poor and as weak as they.

Over the years Mother Teresa's own perception of poverty and suffering has grown. Work in more affluent countries has brought her to the recognition that spiritual poverty, loneliness and the lack of love are far more difficult problems to solve than physical deprivation, and induced her repeatedly to call upon those caught up in the materialism of the West to identify the poverty and the anguish of plenty.

The Sick and Suffering Links include not only the physically sick but also the depressed and the mentally ill. One mentally handicapped child who cannot speak but who somehow manages to make himself understood with his eyes and his smile is linked through his mother to one of the Brothers. To Mother Teresa the world today is an open Calvary. Everywhere there is suffering: the suffering of chronic disease and starvation, and the suffering of niggling aches and unshared sorrows. For some there is suffering simply in solitude or in the knowledge that all things, in time, must crumble and pass away; and for many it is in the mundane discomforts of their daily lives that the drama and the import of a great redemptive passion is most readily lost. The streets of Calcutta lead to Everyman's door, Mother Teresa tells us, and they are trodden by a Christ who, even when he comes amongst his own, remains cruelly unrecognized. Yet her vision is one of hope. For Mother Teresa there is no such thing as an incurable or incorrigible person for through faith and love every situation, no matter how apparently hopeless, contains the embryo of a secret promise. If Christ still suffers in Calcutta, New York, Hong Kong or London, then Christ still saves. The message of Mother Teresa and the many who work with her as representatives of love in the lives of the suffering people, is that deep in the hearts and bodies of humanity Christ is actual and real, and for those prepared to perceive this fact suffering need be neither senseless nor solitary.

2

JACQUELINE DE DECKER
'A life offered joyfully'

> Give yourself fully to God. He will use you to accomplish great things on the condition that you believe much more in his love than in your own weakness.
>
> MOTHER TERESA

Jacqueline de Decker was persuaded to speak about her own life and suffering only as an illustration of how God makes use of otherwise ineffectual instruments and of how suffering can draw an individual closer to his Creator. Jacqueline wears an orthopaedic collar round her neck, her body is encased in an iron corset and she walks with the aid of crutches; but she has unlimited dignity, irrepressible joy and, above all else, an infectious smile. Despite her physical handicap and constant pain she manages to visit and befriend countless other sick people and look after the welfare of approximately a thousand of Antwerp's prostitutes. Yet she is reluctant to talk of her own experiences. To 'wear her heart on her sleeve' is for her one of the most difficult things. 'In a way', she claims, 'it is like being raped', and she looks upon her extraordinary life as a failure transformed into something constructive only by the power and infinite love of God.

My first experience of being asked to accept suffering came when I was fifteen. After a diving accident I experienced considerable pain in my back and I felt that God was asking me to suffer in this way. Even then my response was to accept and so my acceptance of suffering dates back to when I was very young. But I wasn't all that noble. I have to admit that at that time the pain was not all that severe and the doctors had told me that I would be cured by the time I was eighteen!

Nevertheless, even in those days I was beginning to think in terms of going to India. 'There are so many people in the world who suffer', I thought, 'yet God cannot reach them without hands to care for them and feet to go to them.' Why couldn't I be those things? I decided to devote my life to God and to the service of others. I think I was about seventeen or eighteen when I had my vocation – you know, even Mother can't remember exactly when she received her vocation. At a certain moment I took it into my head that I was going to be a missionary nun in order to work in India, so I went along to one of the Belgian convents of the Sisters of Mary to test my vocation. When I arrived there the Sisters put me in a vast part of the convent that was set aside for 'come and sees'. That same evening they gave me tinned salmon for supper and I ate it, not knowing that my stomach was already riddled with fibres. Now I know that I must not touch tinned food of any kind, but in my innocence I ate the salmon with enthusiasm. That night I had a roaring fever, the perspiration poured off me and I was convinced that I would die, all alone in that deserted wing of the convent. Next morning I presented myself to the Mother Superior like a limp rag, and told her I wanted to go home. She assured me that the Sisters would care for me but my mind was made up. I would give myself to God but stay in the world. The tinned salmon had convinced me that I was not meant to go into a convent. In other words, my lay vocation, India, everything, was all due to a poor, or rather a rotten little salmon!

A short time afterwards I joined up with a group of other lay people with similar ideas about doing social work where it was most needed, but then the war interrupted our plans. Two of the other girls who intended to come out to India with me were killed, others decided to get married instead. I too, had to struggle to be true to my vocation. I was often tempted to get married and have children but then I would remind myself: 'I have such a painful back. It would be difficult to be a good wife.' I think in a way my back helped me to have a vocation and, at the same time, having a vocation helped me to carry the cross.

At the end of the war a Jesuit father from Louvain told me

that one of four Jesuit priests booked to sail to India had fallen very ill and would be unable to travel. He invited me to take the sick man's place, assuring me that he would arrange for me to receive the necessary funds, etc. So I left for India at very short notice, quite unprepared for what lay ahead but on the very day that my ship set sail my adviser from Louvain died, and I was left to fend for myself. Still I went to India full of hope and I stayed for more than two years, trying to do whatever I could to start dispensaries, to help the poor or simply to be with some destitute man dying of cholera in the street. I had also to give talks on social work and on why as Christians we should be prepared to help in this way. That I didn't like, because I was hardly equipped to give talks in English in those days. I wasn't starving but my diet was very poor, and the sense of isolation was the worst part of it. I remember one Christmas finding myself walking home all alone after Midnight Mass, knowing that there was nothing for me to eat and consoling myself with the thought of what Jesus Christ's first Christmas must have been like. I look back on it with amusement now, but at the time it was very hard.

Eventually a Jesuit priest in Madras told me about a Sister Teresa who was planning to live and work in much the same way as I was. He suggested that I went to see her, so I went, not without some reservations, to Calcutta to find this little Sister Teresa who was leaving her Convent to be with the poor. She had already left for Patna and so it was in the chapel there that we finally met. Talking together, we discovered that we had the same ideal. She too, was about to be all alone on the streets of Calcutta but she hoped to gather some helpers about her and so we planned that I should join her. But then she was not the Mother Teresa the world acclaims today. She was just a little nun with big ideas and I couldn't help remembering the words of my spiritual director in Antwerp: 'Don't go into a convent. There are many convents in India and you will be tempted to enter one because it seems easier, but you must remain with the poor people.' Sister Teresa had a wonderful idea but there was no guaranteeing that she would actually accomplish it. In a little while she might well be back in a great big cloister with a clanging door and a huge key. I had to admit to her also that my health was very bad. The heat, poor food and Indian transport were causing me terrible problems. I suppose I had been neglecting myself but I could do so no longer. We agreed that it would be sensible for me to return to Belgium to rest and sort out my health difficulties before making any final decision.

On the voyage back to Belgium from India, I was overwhelmed by a sense of failure. My ideal of going to India to work for the poor had failed for a number of reasons . . . the war that broke up our group of lay social workers, the death of the priest who had arranged for me to go out to India, and on top of that, there was my own incapacity to do what I had set out to do. I did many things in India, but in my own eyes, my intentions had not been realized. The desperation that brought me home was moral failure. God had called me to India and I had failed him. For months I could no longer feel his presence despite the fact that I prayed for hours and hours, and I must say that even after all my operations, that was the worst experience I have ever undergone. I stared out of the portholes of the overcrowded old ship and longed to throw myself into the water. I wanted desperately to kill myself. In fact, if it had been left to me, I would have committed suicide, but I was saved because I was made to feel that I still had a place in the world to help others.

Having lost all sense of the presence of God, it came to me one day that Jesus Christ was a living person on earth and that he had a mother. That mother, I felt sure, would understand what I was going through, so I asked our Lady to give me a sign, just some small indication that I was right to come back. With this in mind, when the ship stopped at Marseilles, I disembarked and, instead of returning directly to Antwerp, made my way to Lourdes. (Incidentally, just as a demonstration of how life is, the ship on which I had travelled was shipwrecked in the course of its very next trip, and many of its passengers were drowned. If I had only been on the next voyage, I might have died anyway.)

I went to Lourdes not with the request that I should be cured but rather that our Lady might give me a sign through someone near me. By the time I got there I was the green and yellow colour that people sometimes turn after living in the poor conditions of countries like India, and I was very sick, too sick even to look after myself. Fortunately, as I was crossing the courtyard of a hospital for Belgian pilgrims, a voice suddenly called out to me: 'Jacqueline, what on earth are you doing here?' It was a girl who had done her nursing training with me at Louvain and she recognized instantly that I was not at all well. The Belgian hospital was full to bursting point, as were most of the hospitals in Lourdes, but my friend took me to a hostel she knew a little way out of the town and there arranged for me to share a room with one of the women who ran the place.

While I was resting, suddenly there was a knock at the door. A nurse was needed desperately to sit with one of the pilgrims who was very sick. This woman was apparently raving and violent and must have someone with her constantly; but the woman whose room I was sharing was not a nurse. Quite on impulse I got to my feet and said to them: 'But I am a nurse.' They tried to tell me that I was too ill, but I insisted that it would do me good to do something for somebody else.

The patient was quite mad. She kept muttering obscenities and staring at the windows, wanting to fling herself out of it. She refused all food and medicine but after much persuasion we managed to give her a sleeping tablet in a glass of wine. Eventually she calmed down sufficiently for me to sit with her alone. I could not sleep for thinking of India and so I sat and watched her quietly. Suddenly I thought, 'Hm, we are in Lourdes. She should have a rosary in her hands.' I entwined a rosary round her fingers even as she slept, and waited.

At five o'clock in the morning she woke and announced quite calmly that she was hungry. She had been so completely mad that I couldn't believe her new tranquillity, but she insisted that she was cured. 'I think I said some terrible things', she told me, but I assured her that it was best to forget about what she had said and asked her how it was that she was feeling so much better. 'I must tell you', she said, 'that our Lady came here in the night. I don't know whether it was in my mind or in reality but she was there just in that corner.' When the doctor came, he confirmed the woman's complete recovery. Then he turned to me and shook my hand and congratulated me on having cured her, and it seemed quite extraordinary to me because in India people do not shake hands. The doctor was the first person to shake my hand since I had returned to Europe and I was quite unused to it. Why also did he insist on saying that it was I who had effected the cure? The episode left a deep impression on me and afterwards I was struck by the infinite tenderness of our Lady for listening to my silly talk. I had asked her to give me a sign through someone near to me and she had intervened. It seemed that it was right for me to return to Belgium and the worst of my depression was over.

When I returned to my family in Antwerp, however, life was not particularly easy. My parents belonged to another century. They had nine children and three maids so we did not have a great deal of contact with my father and mother. Nevertheless, they had thought I was quite mad to go out to India in the first place and my illness confirmed all their worst fears. My family too must have felt that I was a failure, so I retreated to the mountains of Switzerland, at first to a kind of retreat house for nurses and then to a hermitage high up in the mountains, run by some Benedictines. I remember climbing and climbing in search of solitude and peace. I went with no food, nothing, and I planned simply to sleep in the open air as I had done so often in India. Naturally I could not sleep in the actual hermitage but there was a small chapel set apart from the main building and I made my home on a narrow bench outside this chapel. I intended just to stay there quietly without food, and pray for as long as was necessary, but the porter who knew that I was there with no food kept bringing me tit-bits – a slice of bread or perhaps a banana. So you see, I had nothing but I received.

After a while I had to give up sleeping on my bench and move down into the village at night, to protect the monks from gossip associated with my presence, but I began my faith anew in the perfect peace of the mountains and that grotto. There calmly and methodically I went through the Creed and found God again.

When I got back to Belgium I saw a specialist about the paralysis that had begun to set in and when they finally X-rayed my back properly, it became apparent that my spine was too badly damaged for me ever to return to India and Mother Teresa's new Order. My doctor did not give an exact name to my disease – I call it the G.G.D. or God Given Disease – but he told me that I must have an operation on my spine. I passed the news on to Mother Teresa and one or two months after my arrival back in Belgium I received a letter from her asking me to offer everything for her and the work and to find others to do the same, and so the Sick and Suffering Link began. It began at the very same time as the first Sisters started to join that solitary little Sister in the slums and it has been growing ever since.

So for me suffering in itself, as Mother Teresa says, was nothing. I was a failure and my suffering was not building anything. On the contrary it was destructive. But suffering shared with the passion of Christ has become a precious gift. The very centre of my life is Jesus Christ and I know that through his passion and the cross comes a message of supreme hope: our redemption through the resurrection. When I seek an explanation for suffering I look at my model Jesus Christ, and when I see him tread the way of Calvary, I know that I must simply follow in his footsteps. I try really to live what Mother Teresa tells us to do: to 'accept what

God gives and what he takes with a big smile'. When I'm in pain, when my back is aching I really feel that I am carrying on my shoulders the cross of Christ and that I must carry it in order to realize in my body what is still necessary in the passion of Christ – in his actual body, which as St Paul says is the Church. I trust and hope in the fact that Jesus has asked me to follow this way, because he said to his disciples: 'If you want to follow me you must take up the cross.'

When we see the cross now we know that Jesus saved mankind through his death, but if we had been there at the time of the crucifixion we would have thought: 'That life is a failure. He did so many wonderful things but now he is hanging on the cross between two thieves.' But as Mother Teresa constantly reminds us, 'God loved the world so much that he gave his only begotten son.' He also told his disciples: 'They persecuted me. They will persecute you.' Thus suffering and failure are a link between the master and the disciple, and are capable of transformation through God's love and the resurrection.

Of course, I too had to go through the passion before I could be resurrected. Jesus in Gethsemane was in agony also and said to his Father: 'Take this cup from me.' I said the same but when Mother Teresa asked for the Sick and Suffering Link I realized how important it was for the Kingdom of God that there was a union between those who suffer and those who are able to be active. Just as action is without importance if it is not shared with the action of Christ; so the same principle may be applied to our suffering.

I could never have imagined that an organization of sick people could help a person to act, but God has used my failure and that of others for his Kingdom and that is wonderful. Everything that I do now – the way that I am in contact with so very many remarkable people, is due to God's using the wretched failure that I am. When we suffer we lose the self to some degree and so God is better able to use us in the way he wants – as Mother Teresa puts it – we become the empty chalice into which God can pour what he wills.

Even my work with the prostitutes was in a way made possible by my handicap. It began when I was in a huge plaster following one of my operations. At that time my brother-in-law, who was a judge, was presiding over a case involving a number of prostitutes in Antwerp, and in the course of questioning one of the girls remarked to him: 'It's all very well for you, but nobody looks after us.' Knowing that I was a trained social worker, my brother-in-law asked me whether I knew of anyone who looked after the interests of prostitutes in the city. I made enquiries on his behalf but there was no one really prepared to help them so I asked my brother-in-law to give me the name of just one of the girls. Naturally, he wasn't supposed to, but I knew that if he would only supply me with one I would be able to find out who the others were. He gave me the name of a girl who was actually awaiting trial and I set out to find her.

By some extraordinary coincidence she was living in a house that had once belonged to my grandmother, but which had been converted into a kind of students' hostel run by nuns. I began to talk to the girl and she was quite obviously all set to moan and complain, when suddenly she broke off: 'But what are you doing here in that enormous plaster?' I explained that I had had an operation but that previously I had been a nurse and a social worker, that now I felt utterly useless but that, having heard that she was looking for a job, I had come to see if I could help her. 'Are you in pain?', she asked me, and when I admitted that I was, she began to try and make me more comfortable. She couldn't get over the fact that despite my own discomfort, I still wanted to help her – and that's how it all started. Because I was handicapped, the girls felt compassion and sympathy for me, and out of that compassion I built a normal and often wonderful relationship. That's what I always do. When I'm with the girls I smoke cigarettes because they do – so why not? Now I have a thousand girls and I'm a grandmother through debauchery a thousand times over. Just think that I was brought up to be so very correct and now I'm surrounded by all the worst stories. I won't say, as Mother Teresa does, that my poor are the redeemers of the world!

I see all this as an illustration of how God can and does act through our very handicaps. The cross is always in my body, I must say, but I can also say that through my suffering I have come to understand the spirit of Jesus Christ much better. I have found too a better understanding of the suffering of others and together we have been able to draw closer to God. This has nothing to do with my merits. Even though I may complain or be impatient or not as charitable as I should be (and I am by no means a saint – sometimes I know that my suffering has made me hard and sometimes I think that if I had been able to be more active, I would have put too much of my own will into God's work) despite all this, God's grace can work through us.

We handicapped people feel very poor, humanly speaking. We may well have lost the use of our hands or legs but faith can be our most precious treasure just as it can be for those who are more active. I remember once when I was in Rome I went to visit a blind couple, and when I knocked at their door, it was opened, apparently by some invisible person. I couldn't see anyone in the doorway because I have difficulty in bending my head but suddenly I heard a little voice saying, 'I'm so happy to see you', and when I managed to look down, I discovered a little dwarf with arms outstretched to greet me and a beaming smile on her face, just as if she were welcoming a prince into the flat. I warmed to her instantly, although I must admit that physically she was not very attractive: her legs and body were all crooked and she was only about as tall as a table. She led me through to the couple I had come to visit and told me with obvious joy: 'They may be blind but I am their eyes.' She explained that previously she had been in a home for destitutes but then, when she heard that two blind people needed help in the home, she had volunteered her services just to be able to be useful to somebody. 'And now', she said, 'it's wonderful because I am actually able to help them.' And the two blind people were equally delighted because they could carry on their work as massage therapists. Together those three people were a full person. Because of their handicap they gave more to others and their happiness communicated itself.

The Sick and Suffering have a wonderful weapon and that is their smile. I visit many sick people and many of them manage to radiate the love of Christ because they smile even through their pain. I have seen thalidomide people with such courage and joy, who think only of others, and I have seen healthy people who think only of themselves. The phrase that Mother Teresa repeats so often, 'God has carved you the palm of his hand', seems particularly wonderful to me because it means that we sick and handicapped people have no need to fear, no reason not to smile.

Two of the principal sources of inspiration for the Sick and Suffering Link are those wonderful words of Cardinal Newman's prayer, 'penetrate and possess my whole being so utterly that all my life may be only a radiance of thine', and the changing of the water into wine at the wedding feast in Cana. We must seek purity of spirit and be prepared to be changed by Jesus Christ into good red wine.

The Gospel also tells us that we are all given talents and in a sense our suffering is our talent but we should beware of paying too much attention to it and try to keep a sense of proportion about our physical disabilities. Mother Teresa always insists on respect for life, even the life of a child born severely crippled, and so if we become crippled we must continue to respect our bodies and do for them what we as humans beings would do for another cripple. As a nurse I must care for my own body but only to the extent that is really necessary, not to the extent of considering the doctor's efforts insufficient. Finding the balance between doing what God wants us to do for our bodies and over-doing concern for our own wellbeing, is never easy. For me it was always difficult to decide when I should have an operation. My doctor did not make the decision. I had to tell him when the pain had become unbearable because each time he opened me up, there was always the risk that the operation itself would cause more fibres to grow and so result in worse paralysis.

What we sick people must concentrate on is going deeper and deeper into the life of Christ. I am reminded of someone I shall refer to only as the 'malcontent'. I often visit her, trying to help her, trying to distract her as she struggles against the pain. She finds her own uselessness tiresome. She feels that no doctor can really understand her illness and that no medicine can really be of any use to her. She cannot sleep properly. She is on a tedious diet because she is too fat and she complains constantly because she has no visitors. In short, nothing is right for her.

I would love to write her a letter to help her discover all God's loving concern for her. Does she not have a good and devoted therapist? If she could only thank that therapist with a big smile, she would make her very happy. And that doctor bowed over her suffering, is he not part of God's care? Does she ever think of their tiredness at the end of the day while she has been resting all day long? Does she think to pray for them?

Somehow she simply does not see how spoilt she is by the compassion and help of a friend who comes daily to visit her and do her shopping. Does she think to pray for her? Do we ever think of praying for the doctor when we go for a consultation so that the Holy Spirit may guide him in his diagnosis and choice of treatment. Instead of being anxious or impatient in the doctor's waiting room, why don't we pray silently for each of the patients waiting beside us.

When Jesus Christ hung motionless on the cross, apparently useless, he was saving us. Our uselessness should be an opportunity to discover all the values that people, caught up in the rush and bustle of work, cannot do: the value of silence, of listening, of the beauty of nature, the value of other people – of joy and suffering, the value of medicine and even of dieting – as a form of sacrifice.

It is true that in the beginning God created a clean, whole-some nature, devoid of sickness or sorrow, but we human beings changed it. We introduced pollution, alcoholism, drugs and a multitude of evils, for which we have to find remedies. So why not do as Mother Teresa does? Each time she drinks a glass of water or takes a mouthful of food she blesses it with the sign of the cross.

Why should we become anxious about every petty pain or symptom, imagining that we must have leukaemia or cancer at the very least? Let us have peaceful hearts and arm ourselves with courage, trusting in God and in the knowl-edge that even if we do fall ill, he will give us the necessary strength to cope. After all, so very many others have had to struggle with such illnesses and have managed to turn them into a grace, so why should we not be able to do likewise?

Why also should we be bitter when someone looks at our handicap and shows compassion? Do you think we don't need compassion? Did not Jesus himself have compassion for the hungry crowd beside the sea of Galilee? And in his compassion he multiplied the five loaves and two fishes into enough food to fill the multitudes. Pity is an outreaching of the heart towards the suffering of others. It is up to the one who suffers to accept it and transform it into a compassion compiled from mutual love.

There is so much strength to be received in the Eucharist where Christ again offers us his broken body, and so much can be achieved by prayer. The sick can use their hours of sleeplessness, those empty early morning hours when no one else is yet awake, for silent adoration. When Mother Teresa had over a month in hospital in Rome she spent a whole hour of each morning and each afternoon in adora-tion before the Host. Prayer and meditation can bring unfathomable consolation. 'When it is very hard for you', Mother Teresa once wrote, 'hide yourself in the Sacred Heart.'

We must have courage and trust. God does not remove all difficulties and pain in life with the stroke of some mysterious magic wand. Rather he invites man to dive resolutely into the uncertainty of life with the sole certainty that God is in the very depths and that in those same depths lie the revelation and realization of love.

Those who suffer can reflect more faithfully the image of Christ. Many of the Sick and Suffering feel so united with the passion that they suffer more acutely during Holy Week. With Christ they learn what it is to be betrayed, ignored, misunderstood and in pain. Thus Jesus is crucified and resurrected again in those who suffer.

I have known people who had the stigmata and I know that it is good for me to see people suffering the passion of Christ. To me Lourdes, the Eucharist, the Sick and Suffering, people who have the stigmata – they are all one. They are the actual passion of Christ, but I must say that the supernatural part of belief has nothing to do with my faith. If you told me tomorrow that one of those stigmatized people was a fraud I would say quite simply: 'All right – that's his or her affair.'

Many people experience a kind of conversion in their lives. Suddenly they experience an extraordinary inner light. That is a special grace, although I suppose that God may well grant such graces to many who simply choose not to accept them. One can tell whether such experiences are valid only by whether the joy, the light and the love are afterwards borne out in the life of the individual concerned.

Mother Teresa has said that when my suffering increases she experiences an increase in energy. I suppose too that there have been some extraordinary coincidences in our lives but I do not, for example, have presentiments about her being ill. I am ill because she must not be, and on the whole she has been exceptionally healthy. But for the time during which Mother was in hospital in Rome I had the grace to be twinned with her suffering. I had serious spine troubles and terrible pain until the day when Mother came out of hospital. Then my suffering was relieved. God has been good to us, helping us to share his cross for the world of today.

All those, regardless of their creed, who are completely willing to do God's will receive in a certain way the marks of the cross. God loves everyone and God wishes to redeem each one of us through Christ, and so a Hindu or Muslim, etc. who follows God's life in him can still find his way to God through Christ, though he may not recognize or know Christ's way.

Nor is suffering, of course, the privilege of the faithful. Suffering has nothing to do with God; it is part of our human nature – so much so that when Christ came into the world he had to suffer. God could have redeemed the world by appearing as a ray of sunshine, a beautiful flower or an awesome apparition, but he chose to come as just an ordinary man. Imagine that people actually spat in his face – to me that is one of the worst things. He took the blow of a common soldier and the jeers of the masses. He accepted all that just to show that he knew that suffering was part of being human and to teach us how to accept and transcend it.

When I am with someone who is suffering without faith, I appeal to their human dignity. Why, I ask them, should they refuse to accept suffering when so many others have had to suffer terribly? To suffer bravely and unselfishly, I tell them, is to be a good man – it is to demonstrate the very best in our humanity and, at the very least, it can teach us how to love each other better.

3

THE SICK AND
SUFFERING CO-WORKERS

'Suffering borne together is joy'

Jesus said to the people of his time: 'If you want to be my disciples take up the cross and follow me.'

A priest of the Community of the Resurrection writes of the mysterious paradox of goodness found in evil, the same paradox which suggests that death can cure and sickness strengthen, and which enables those who suffer to become people who, with a courageous smile, bring joy to the world and lend energy to the thrust of life:

I would like to say something about the goodness of evil. It is not that I think there can be any goodness in sin but rather in all those things – pain, loneliness, sickness, poverty, hunger, persecution and death make up part of what is called 'the problem of evil'.

Who can find any goodness in any of these? And the answer is the man and woman who take up their cross and follow after Christ, for it is thereby that they become his disciples, and as his disciples they can learn not only the reality of suffering, but also the reality of the resurrection, which is life with Christ, and in Christ.

When our Lord told his disciples to take up their cross, we must remember that the cross had not been sentimentalized; it was a grim symbol of disgrace, of long drawn out agony, of ugliness and of death. So it is as though our Lord had said, 'Follow me, and this is all the thanks you can expect'.

When our Lord died, he made the one perfect and sufficient sacrifice for the sins of the whole world. His death and his resurrection are the only effective instruments of man's salvation, and this is ever to be borne in mind. So what possible use is my bearing a cross? The Christian who accepts sickness, poverty, and even misunderstanding and reproach as being his cross, is joining himself to all the saints and martyrs who have suffered for Christ's sake. St Paul dared to say, 'I rejoice in my sufferings. I complete what is lacking in Christ's affliction' (Col. 1.24). What is there lacking? The sacrifice is complete, but its full effectiveness depends not just on the goodness of God, but on the response of men, and its effectiveness is increased by the generosity of the attitude of all the saints, and of humble people, like us. And surely it is increased because we are one Body with Christ, and with all his Church, the Apostles, the martyrs, and all the confessors, the people who 'stand up to be counted'. One Body, one Blood with him, so that at last there is a perfect unity, which is nourished by the richness of the full-grown individuality of each of us. This unity is enriching us, and our own individuality is enriching the whole.

Having written all this, I look back on my own life, with a certain misgiving. My life has been a happy one, and any cross I have had to bear has been a light one, suited, perhaps, to my little strength. For it may be that at the end of the day what will matter will be the quality of our faith, whether it will have been purified, deepened and strengthened, or whether it will have been washed all away, like the house built on the sands. It is that end product that matters. 'Take my yoke upon you, and learn of me, for I am gentle and lowly of heart, and you will find rest for your souls. For my yoke is easy, and my burden is light' (Matt. 11.29).

Suffering by itself is nothing but suffering shared with Christ's passion is a wonderful gift to human life. It is the most beautiful gift that we can share in the passion of Christ.

MOTHER TERESA

Many of the letters of the sick to the Sisters or Brothers with whom they are linked, betray an instant and intuitive understanding of that mysterious vocation to which Mother Teresa has said they are called.

One Sick and Suffering Co-worker had been suffering from multiple sclerosis for nineteen years. It began when she was only twenty-one years old and studying at university and so, instead of helping the sick as she had wanted, she became an invalid herself and had to learn to accept helplessness. She was married with two children, but her husband left her and her children were taken away from her because she was unable to care for them. Yet, even after such anguish, she was able to say: 'I have no gold, no money but what I have – a broken body, my thoughts and my prayers – that is my offering.' To the Sisters with whom she is linked, she wrote:

Did you know that you had an adoptive Sister? Here I am longing with all my heart to work with you, to tend Jesus Christ's suffering body in all the miserable poor you care for. Like Jacqueline de Decker I was once a nurse and am now an invalid due to multiple sclerosis.

It was marvellous to discover that sickness, even the kind that keeps you in bed, need not stop you working. Love, much love, opens the way to another life and gives so much joy and peace and health of heart and soul. Of course, there are difficult moments. It is by no means an easy way but our Lord's hand is leading us and helps us to our feet whenever we stumble or fall.

I want to tell you how happy I am to have a Sister with whom I can work so that my life is not wasted or lost, but full of the work I love so much.

Despite partially paralysed hands, she also wrote to Jacqueline de Decker:

In our pathetic mediocrity Mother Teresa asks us to transform suffering into joy, a deep joy. To satiate the thirst of Jesus for souls – what a grace, what riches. It is in this way that God involves us in his work. It is so important for me to be linked with a Missionary of Charity, otherwise what meaning can I give to my illness? It is only the Lord who can transform our pains into an offering.

My path is rocky but full of flowers – those little humble flowers that you don't notice if you can run. When the journey is hard let us link hands. Friendship is the sharing of great things and the patient care of doctors, nurses and priests eases my pain. So it is that God gives back a hundred-fold what he takes from me.

When the time comes and we cannot pray, it is very simple – let Jesus pray in us to the Father in the silence of our hearts. If we cannot speak, he will speak. If we cannot pray, he will pray. So let us give him our inability and our nothingness.

MOTHER TERESA

To suggest that there are those who are able to accept the role of 'living with Jesus on the cross every day' so readily is not to lose sight of all the pain, the heartbreak and the doubts. Many refer to times when they cannot 'accept', times when they cannot even pray. To these people Mother Teresa brings the firm assurance that perfect prayer does not consist of many words but of the fervour of the desire which raised the heart of Jesus Christ . . .

Forgive my long silence. I am not particularly proud of myself. I was delighted when you gave me the name of the Brother with whom I was to be linked, and had every intention of writing to him and praying in union with him.

Then suddenly I felt so discouraged and something in me refused to pray. I felt paralysed, incapable of praying, and this went on for months. I began to doubt the truth of God and tried to forget my illness and my suffering by shaking off all thoughts about it and just being happy with anything and everything. But I found only a great emptiness, and self-deception; and I came back and threw myself in the arms of the Lord knowing that he alone *is*.

Since then I have rediscovered my peace and despite my illness, suffering and solitude, I am happy and want to share my offering so that the Lord may help my fellow-man, may help the Brother whom God has entrusted to me.

Yes, now I am really on his side. I offer myself and pray that God may send him all the grace he needs; and I am actually with him amongst the poor and the sick for whom he cares.

Our lives are utterly wasted if we use only the light of reason. Our life has no meaning unless we look at Christ in his poverty.

MOTHER TERESA

In 1954 Jacqueline de Decker wrote to Pope Pius XII to tell him that some of the Sick and Suffering Co-workers were praying for him, and out of this letter sprang the idea of linking a number of the sick specifically to the Pope. One of these links was an English woman disabled by polio in her childhood and later more acutely handicapped by a series of strokes. She also suffered from diabetes and failing eyesight. In 1980 she wrote of her difficulties in adjusting from a relatively active life as a doctor to that of an invalid in a wheelchair:

45

You see when one becomes disabled, 'struck down', as some people like to say, especially when one has led a pretty active life, then one is beset by the 'do-gooders' and the 'holy hens' telling one to 'accept' and 'offer up' this truly awful, unreal event in one's life. I had been quite severely disabled since an attack of polio in 1947 but to find myself in a home for incurables was something completely different. The name alone was enough to give me the horrors. The first six months were hell, in a room with five others who were much older than me and who had been there for many years. One was almost told when one should breathe and around they all came with their 'offering' and 'accepting'. I couldn't, of course, no one can at first. I couldn't see even the light at the end of the tunnel for about six months. Then, gradually, dimly one saw some sort of pattern.

Slowly, slowly when I heard about some awful happening in the world I would try to say a prayer. It was all that I could do really, for I was poor in the fullest sense of the word. Then came the idea that when someone was in particular need I could make a silent promise not to grumble or complain about anything for so many hours or even for a day. Because of my partial blindness it was difficult for me to write to a Sister – I was using all my physical energy on working for an Open University degree – but it was suggested to me that I should 'just pray for the Pope'.

I lost my heart to Pope John Paul I for his smile and the rakish angle of his skull cap. Pope John Paul II captured it by rushing across Rome regardless of everyone and everything to see his sick friend. I will be totally blind soon but he makes things very easy for me because I can appreciate his yearning for his homeland, his essential apartness, his understanding of the cares of the world and his private longing to be alone to pray. It is not difficult to offer one's blindness and prayers for a man like that!

It is not how much we do that is pleasing to God, but how much love we put into the doing. Together let us build a chain of love around the world.

MOTHER TERESA

From Brazil a man who is hemiplegic on the left side of his body writes the following:

Speaking as a handicapped person, I should like to direct some words of encouragement, coming from the bottom of my heart, to those who carry a heavy cross through life, but try to transform that cross into an instrument of faith, through which suffering becomes ever less painful.

We know that man is a chronically unsatisfied creature. His emotional instability is reflected back to him, as it were, from all that life brings to him, especially suffering. When pressurized by the anguish of pain, some men revert to sadness, others to fear, others allow themselves to be dominated by anger directed against all and everyone. Few accept suffering with faith. Faith, however, is able to bring even suffering within the level of our energies. St Paul wrote, in his First Epistle to the Corinthians (10.13) that God will ask of no one that which it is beyond his ability to bear.

It is also important to bear in mind that suffering is not something exclusively mine or yours, but of all men. Pain has always been a constant factor in everyone's life. When it is not a paralysis immobilizing his members, an affliction in the organs, an illness robbing him of his sight, it is an inner problem touching his soul. All are without distinction found out by suffering. When our pain becomes more intense, we may hope to free ourselves somewhat from our egoism and realize that someone, perhaps even close by, may be suffering more. If one's egoism does not allow one to feel a neighbour's anguish, one may still bow before

Christ, the greatest martyr, daily crucified by ungratefulness, sin and man's depravity. Christ is a crystal mirror for all men.

I see Christ in the ill, the beggar, the prisoner . . . I know that some day he'll say: 'Come, ye blessed of my Father, inherit the kingdom prepared for you from the foundation of the world: for I was hungry and you gave me food. I was thirsty and you gave me drink. I was a stranger and you welcomed me, naked and you clothed me. I was ill and you comforted me, in prison and you came to visit me' (Matt. 25. 31–40). This is the spiritual importance of suffering: Christ lives more in the sick, the beggars, the imprisoned, the wanderers.

There are those who see suffering more as a consequence of our sins or defects of our parents. But Christ was very clear on this point, in St John's Gospel (9. 1–3) where Christ is asked about a man blind from birth and his disciples asked him, 'Rabbi, was it his sin or that of his parents that caused him to be blind?' 'Neither', answered Jesus, 'It was no sin of this man's nor of his parents. Rather it was to let God's works show forth in him.'

Though the suffering be hard, uncomfortable, heavy, there is something of the divine in it: the manifestation of God before man for the future heavenly Kingdom!

When great torment makes one wish for death, one should not be egoistic to the point of forgetting others. Pain is the instrument of redemption and love. It demands sacrifice, detachedness, and giving, but is repaid with sublime sentiments.

God the Father, in order to save mankind, gave his son Jesus Christ to be crucified. And Jesus accepted the cross and its consequences, in spite of man's ingratitude and meanness.

Thus I try to give the greatest value to my suffering. I am sure it is a treasure with which I am building a stair to eternity on which my brother may climb, and I and all men desirous of reaching God.

Nothing is more able to console me than to know that my

suffering is a divine manifestation, renewing me, leading me to God. It is divine as is the magnificence of the universe, the purity of a child, the beauty of art, the shapeliness of flowers, the brilliance of lightning, the sound of thunder.

God is a loving Father, a merciful Father who wishes us a Kingdom of glory, forever, free from tears, sacrifice and pain, where the victory over death is complete. 'He shall wipe every tear away from the eyes; and there shall be no more death, neither sorrow nor crying, neither shall there be any more pain: for the former things are passed away' (Rev. 21.4).

We should be ingenuous to think that God created man to live merely twenty, fifty or ninety years. Human life is sublime and becomes complete life when united with God and eternity. For the Christian with faith there is no death; this life is only a passage to a new existence. Have no fear of life's culminating instant. We should think of death as a dedicated friend, anxious to open for us the door to the Kingdom of God. In this life, Christ is our force and the holy Virgin Mary our consolation. Saint Theresa of Jesus tells us that the cross, when dragged, is heavy; when embraced, however, it is light.

Why then, brother sufferer mine, be led into despair and disillusionment when you may easily become an intermediary between your neighbour and the Father?

Strengthen yourself with prayer, allowing prayer to take the place of tears and depression. Let us unite our prayers and our hopes towards the building of a world of peace and love. Let us make a chain of love, transforming our suffering into a source of living waters where those thirsty for justice and faith may satisfy themselves.

> Suffering is a sign of love because this is how God the Father proved that he loved the world – by giving his Son to die for us and expiate our sin.
>
> MOTHER TERESA

Kiki was one of Jacqueline de Decker's 'girls', whose life story she cites as an example of faith rediscovered through suffering and true friendship:

When I first visited Kiki, she was in gaol. I was a prison visitor and she had been sentenced to one year. Originally she had been a typist and then a model, but then she had answered an advertisement, initially believing herself to be applying for a job as a fashion model, and found herself employed as a prostitute. Eventually she was sentenced to gaol for running a brothel.

When she was released in 1961 I helped her to start work again as a proper model but she had run up substantial debts and she had a young daughter. Her husband, who was killed in a car crash, had been an Italian, and so after a while she went to Italy. There she caught diphtheria and pulmonary tuberculosis and had to go to a sanatorium in Switzerland for treatment. Kiki herself nearly died and while she was so dangerously ill, her daughter who was suffering from bouts of depression threw herself out of a fourth-storey window. The girl was not killed but her brain was damaged and she had to spend long periods in a psychiatric institute.

Nevertheless, since I had given her my friendship Kiki had begun to think about God again. 'God has perhaps arranged all this in advance;' she wrote, 'continue to be my friend and help me in this new life and I promise you that I will try to be worthy of your friendship. Perhaps God will make up to me for all the tears I have shed in my life. God put you in my path for you are my one true friend.'

Kiki began to pray again. In the sanatorium she went to confession and to communion. 'Now life has really started', she said, 'I need your prayers. I have rediscovered the God of my childhood and I want to do beautiful things with my life.' But in the sanatorium she had no visitors and sometimes she felt lonely and disheartened. 'I suffer not so much from the treatment', she told me, 'as from the loneliness.'

Her doctor wrote and told me that her lungs were severely damaged. She felt old and empty and inevitably sometimes she rebelled. Yet she had begun to understand that the love of God calls for a response and a response that is wholehearted. She still felt herself to be in a tunnel but she knew that at the end of it there was light and asked for my hand to guide her in the right direction.

'The doctor is talking about taking my lung out', she wrote to me once with utter horror but then one morning she seemed to feel the presence of God and she was able to accept everything. She became calm and peaceful. At the end of 1968 her lungs began to bleed again. Understandably she was discouraged and she suffered a great deal from the cold in the mountains, but she wrote: 'Patience, I have begun to know how to suffer for God who has been so good to me, despite all my sins against him. Pray for my daughter. She hasn't spoken to me for three years. She reproaches me for my former life. I am trying to understand my poor child. After all, she cannot really judge at her age.' The reason for the girl's suicide attempt was epilepsy, from which the doctors said they would never be able to cure her.

Kiki begged for prayers, for money, for clothes, for letters. In between her epileptic attacks, her daughter assured her of her love. The daughter was to have a brain operation and she was understandably frightened at the prospect. For Kiki this was a period of sheer martyrdom but she agreed to adopt a Missionary of Charity Sister and her daughter wanted to do likewise. 'The work of Mother Teresa is so wonderful', Kiki wrote to me. 'How I envy those Sisters who spend their lives alleviating suffering and how I regret having closed my ears to the call of God when I was young. I would still love to do so much for others but I can only pray and ask God to give me moral strength, total forgetfulness of self and a greater capacity for love.'

At Easter I received another letter: 'I am in a convent for a rest. The other day I had a surprise visit from a friend of the Mother Abbess. She came laden with presents and I could not help weeping for joy. God made me feel that at least I am not alone. I have these Sisters, the love of my daughter, you, the abundant love of God and the privilege to be called to suffer for him.

'I am a little better and, joy of all joys, the doctor says that my daughter too could be cured, in a matter of months. I want to tell you about my decision to consecrate myself completely to God. Don't think it has been easy to say "Yes" to the voice of God deep within me. I wanted to kick against it, but it was greater than my weakness – and I have decided that once my daughter no longer needs me, I will go into a convent.'

In July 1970, despite or perhaps because of the fact that she herself was still very ill and her daughter was still suffering from depressions and epileptic attacks, it was Kiki who was able to help me through a series of difficulties that arose in connection with my work amongst the prostitutes. 'Jesus granted you this painful trial', she assured me, 'just to draw you closer to him but he will never abandon you. Your apostolate is a splendid one for what would have become of me, if it had not been for you? Leave the devil to do his mischief. Jesus was subject to the same trials but he conquers all his adversaries. This struggle will only prove your love for the poor prostitutes, for God never makes us suffer for nothing.'

Kiki began a new phase in her life. For three months she worked in a hospital in the mountains and began to train as an assistant nurse: 'Now here in the hospital I have begun the most wonderful work of my life. Every sick person I nurse is Jesus to me. There are so many people suffering from cancer, from old age and from all the other diseases that beset humanity! I pray God that he will give me the strength to do this work.'

'I have a dream', she told me some time later, 'a dream that one day, when she is better, my daughter might come and work with me. We must leave this dream to divine providence.' But by this time her daughter was in a mental asylum and Kiki did not know which way to turn: 'I still don't know what God wants of me – should I continue to work here in the hospital or go into a convent? How can I escape the burden of my past? I am paying heavily for my previous mistakes, but I do so want to deserve your friendship, and I am sure that God will help me despite all the sacrifices he asks of me. I would like at least to end my days bringing love to all those who suffer. I want to offer my suffering to relieve the suffering of others. I am still able to do some good but I need your friendship.

In January 1971 Kiki's daughter again tried to commit suicide after attempting to strangle three nurses. Kiki, having herself just recovered from an attack of bronchitis, went to visit her – 'I was able even to take her out to a restaurant and to the hairdressers. She seemed quite cheerful and did not even mention her suicide attempt, but I am like a dead person. Only my sick people help me to forget. I carry my daughter in my heart and I will continue to fight for her. God will not let me down. Today one of my patients, realizing that he was dying, asked for the very first time to see a priest. He made his confession, received Communion and died in peace – so if God wants my suffering to save souls, may his will be done.'

Months later Kiki's daughter seemed much better: 'She has won a prize for poetry', wrote Kiki, 'and I feel very proud of her. She even wants to start her studies again . . . but that will cost money and I have none to spare. Because I haven't yet taken my diploma I can do only the most disagreeable tasks here, and I have to take the brunt of any mistakes that are made. Sometimes I am reduced to tears, but then if I accept everything humbly I am accused of wanting to be a martyr. Nevertheless, if God wants all this, I place myself in his hands.'

In the summer of 1971 I heard from her again: 'I was full of hope. My daughter was much better and I was promised the opportunity to do proper nurse's work. Then out of the blue, I received a phone call telling me that my daughter was undergoing an operation. She had swallowed her rosary. I went dashing to her, only to find that she was all right. Probably she swallowed the rosary as a cry for my attention. I ask God to give me the courage to go on. My health, at least, is not too bad but I have to take so many medicines and the doctor tells me that I won't be able to go on like this for very long.'

She remained concerned for my welfare. 'Why', she asked, 'is God demanding so much suffering from you – always these operations? God's love is a mystery. I have to learn to love Jesus Christ on the cross. My soul is still in turmoil but I know in my heart of hearts that God is there, and that he guides my life. He knows for what purpose I was born and I must leave everything in his hands. I say to him repeatedly, "Do what you, in your divine love, want with me but please do not leave me alone. Draw me close to you and forgive me my weaknesses and failings."

'My only encouragement here is the gratitude of all my patients – I have learnt to work purely for the love of God.'

At the age of twenty Kiki's daughter became engaged to be married. She was full of hopes and plans for the future but she was still ill and her behaviour was totally unpredictable. Kiki herself suffered from a series of illnesses. We had kept in touch with letters and phone calls and other Co-workers had been able to help in very practical ways. Then, in the winter of 1973 Kiki fell down the stairs.

'I have a bruised rib which has given me an acute attack of asthma. I feel overwhelmed by suffering, but my daughter is very much better. She actually came and looked after me for five days. I would like so much to be able to give my life for the recovery of my daughter.'

The daughter's epilepsy became so bad that it placed a severe strain on her heart. She continued to be moved in and out of hospital and mental institutions. Sometimes she was openly hostile towards her mother, while Kiki continued to suffer courageously and offer her suffering for her Missionary Sister. She had ever more frequent attacks of asthma and bronchitis. She also had a weak heart. Sometimes she would lapse into a coma and sometimes it was simply a sense of solitude that caused her most pain. Yet through all this she managed to continue to hope, and not without some fulfilment, for she achieved her nursing certificate and her daughter became engaged once more. 'I must try to fill my emptiness with a more complete love for God', Kiki told me, 'and I will consecrate my life to those who suffer. I must continue to smile and help my patients and so show them that God is good, his love is immense – he is forgiveness and love.'

When I last heard from her, she was having radiography treatment on her back: 'My disease is gaining ground', she wrote, 'and I have to have oxygen twice a day, but I am in the hands of God so I do not complain. Thank you for teaching me how to suffer for a cause so dear to the heart of Christ – the work of Mother Teresa. I have good news. My daughter is actually getting married on 1st May. I can bear all my suffering since it pays for my daughter's happiness. Even though the price is very high – my neck, my back, my lump, my asthma – I will not be sad. I will continue to love Jesus Christ and suffer with him and in him.'

> The more we empty ourselves, the more room we give God to fill us.
>
> MOTHER TERESA

A French woman with a special love for the natural world regards her suffering as a means of purification and self-mastery:

Together with my sister, who is ten years older than me and also unmarried, I was able to build a little house in the middle of a forest. It was just like Snow White's cottage, surrounded by squirrels, crickets, hedgehogs and all kinds of birds, even owls and particularly barn owls that squabbled from dawn till dusk. There were nightingales too, with their nocturnal songs, and I must not forget creatures like the timid little viper or the grass snake with its extraordinary necklace. All the residents of this little world were so used to us that they even dared to venture into the dining room. Sometimes they would try to perch on the chandelier and come tumbling to the floor.

My sister and I worked in a Social Security Office in a small town, six miles from this little home of ours. As a child I loved God although I was not born into a particularly Christian family. After my first Communion which I didn't make until I was fifteen years old, I had some years of grace, united with the Lord. Later, however, I became unfaithful, ungrateful and abandoned him.

What great misfortunes arise when we abandon God! How rapidly we lapse into darkness and death of the soul. But Jesus Christ was still there. Humbly he was waiting at the door of my heart and his call became more and more persistent.

In 1975 while we were on holiday in the Alps, I went to

Sunday Mass and there I dedicated myself to the Blessed Virgin, asking her to help me rediscover a life of purity and union with the Lord, such as I had experienced on the day of my first Communion. The following December I became very ill and for me that was the beginning of greater detachment from the pleasures of this world. I was thirty-three years old.

How much physical and mental suffering, how many tumbles and tears I have had to go through, how many renouncements I have had to make during these last seven years. Yet how much grace I have experienced also – how much of the Lord's delicacy, for God is not mean with his graces when his poor creatures call upon him and give themselves to him in abandonment and love.

Eventually I was compelled to give up the classical dancing that I loved so much. On January 1, 1976 I burnt my dancing pumps on the fire because I knew I would never dance again. Then, in December of the same year, we had to leave our little house and the beautiful garden in which I had so loved to work, and move into a furnished studio flat in the south of France.

In 1977 my sister had to leave me to go and work in Normandy and I was left on my own, knowing nobody. When I became an 'invalid', I felt as if I was being rejected by society and as if I could no longer be useful to anyone. But after a time God made me understand that, on the contrary, I could now serve him better in my brothers – first by prayer, then by offering up my sufferings and by performing humble tasks for those around me. I made him a promise: that I would never waste my pension money but that I would use as much as possible of it to help those in distress.

One day my sister gave me a little book about Mother Teresa and I wrote to the 'Amis de Mère Teresa' in France. That was how I learnt about Mother Teresa's work and became a Sick and Suffering Co-worker. I asked to be God's little light, just like the candles that children kindle before the crib on Christmas Eve, his little light of love and care for others, for the world needs so much love and tenderness. I did not ask him to cure me because if he did I would have nothing to offer. Without my suffering all my actions would be so poor and so altered by imperfection and sin. Without the cross I might perhaps go astray again. Now I live in peace and am happy to be united with his Sacred Heart for he is the most faithful and most loving partner that any heart could desire.

My greatest yearning is to make him loved and to bring him many souls for the Love that created the squirrels and the nightingales is not loved, and our lady is so forgotten. If only all the people of the world would hold hands with each other we could do such beautiful things for the Lord.

God is still love. He is still loving the world. God loved the world so much that he gave his Son and today God loves the world so much that he gives you, he gives me to love the world – to be his love and his compassion.

MOTHER TERESA

It was an old man who had fought in two world wars and suffered brutal injuries in the process, who provided the reminder that the religious conviction of being loved is in itself therapeutic. 'But', he insisted, 'the great thing is that the initial awakening has nothing to do with great efforts on our part. St John tells us quite explicitly: 'In this is love, not that we loved God but that he loved us' (1 John 4.10). Everything begins with an experience of God's love for us, an experience of grace to which we are invited to respond. Naturally such an experience can be very emotional, but sometimes too we penetrate a little further into the great reality of the risen Christ. In that way our response to love is therapeutic also, for our responding love is not directed at some nebulous abstraction but at the living, cosmic Christ who is in our friends, our enemies, the healthy and the sick. The process of being loved and at the same time, loving God both as himself and in others cannot fail to purify.'

Dolly was a prostitute in Antwerp, whom Jacqueline de Decker met while working as a member of a team of the Legion of Mary:

We met Dolly for the first time in 1970. We had been doing this work since 1956 and we knew more than a thousand prostitutes. It was one of the other girls who told us that Dolly was ill but that she was not really looking after herself. That first visit was by no means a success. She was abrupt with us and did not really want our company, but on our second visit she welcomed us more warmly. We explained to her that we came to give her friendship. Eventually she told us that she had a disease of the throat caused by too much smoking. The doctor had told her that she should have an operation but she was afraid and in any case, she had no money to pay for it. By this time she was sixty-eight years old and had run out of money but she did have deep ray treatment and it became apparent that she had cancer of the throat.

In January she began to choke and suffocate and had to be hurried to the hospital where the doctor performed a tracheotomy. We visited her twice a week and a real friendship developed out of those visits. When she was finally able to go home, her life had changed. She lived in a small room on her social security money. In her poverty she humbly accepted our help with clothes and food. She had a tube in her throat and could not speak properly but somehow we understood her.

Dolly recognized that it was love that we had for her and a love that was different from the kind she was used to, because it was an extension of God's love for her. Eventually she agreed to see a priest and began to pray. 'I am now so overjoyed to have faith', she told us. 'When I look back on my past I am sad but I don't dwell on it now. I can look to the future with hope because I know that God has compassion and has forgiven my faults. I want now to do good for others. I know that I had a bad character. I rebelled against my mother when I was a child. I got married to get away from home and after six weeks I walked out on my husband. I went to Paris and there became a prostitute.'

Often she used to pop into a chapel near her room to pray. On that first Christmas of her conversion she decided to go to midnight Mass and afterwards she told us. 'When I entered the church I was suddenly filled with such great internal joy, such a warm feeling, just as if God himself was filling my heart and I started to cry. But the tears were tears of joy.'

After that experience her spiritual life increased. She became spiritually linked with one of Mother Teresa's Sisters, and in this way she had an actual reason for offering up her suffering.

Very soon she had to undergo another operation, but this time she was able to say: 'I am very peaceful. If God calls me back to him, I know that you will say Mass for the repose of my soul.' The operation was successful. When a friend suggested that she went to a bar for a drink, she refused. When a client met her and offered her money, again she refused.

She tried to live frugally on her allowance in her small room in the red light district of Antwerp. 'I want all the "girls" to see how happy I am now', she insisted. One day a prostitute was ill and Dolly went to visit her in hospital, but the girl had already died. Dolly offered to pay for her funeral Mass. Another day she heard that her last pimp was ill and she went to visit him just to try and show what faith and her love could do. Eventually it became apparent that the man was dying and it was Dolly who rushed out to find a priest to give him the sacrament of the sick. Her ex-pimp died at peace with God. Again she wanted to pay for a Mass for him but she told the priest: 'I am poor'. His answer, 'God came especially for the poor', filled her with joy. When she went to sort out the dead man's sick insurance, by mistake she handed over with his papers a note about the price of his funeral mass. The official handed it back to her, saying rudely: 'We don't reimburse that sort of thing here', but she answered promptly: 'I know but it will be reimbursed in heaven'.

As she was now suffering from arthritis, she was sent into an old people's home. It was not very pleasant for her because she had such an independent nature but she accepted it as the will of God and her smile conquered all. The doctor was so satisfied with her cure that he wanted to remove the tube in her throat with a small operation. She went back into hospital but there, on the second day, she died peacefully in her sleep.

Her funeral Mass was attended by many of the girls from the prostitutes' quarter and a memorial speech was read: 'Dear Dolly, you have left us for a better world but you have left us a precious inheritance – your example, because when you became ill you discovered God and you tried to live your life in accordance with your faith in him. You put all your trust in him. You read the words of St John's Gospel, "Everyone who believes in him shall not perish but have everlasting life" (John 3.16), and you understood that your new master, Jesus Christ, was obedient even unto death, and so transcended the passion and the cross. He accepted suffering in reparation for your sin and for the sins of others because God sent his Son into the world not to condemn it but to save it. That faith, that suffering and that interior peace that was visible on your face and in your smile did us so much good, and you wanted to communicate that faith to others. As Jesus rose again after his passion and death so you too will rise again through him to God.'

Some call him Ishwar, some call him Allah, some simply God, but we all have to acknowledge that it is he who made us for greater things.

MOTHER TERESA

The following extract comes from a Hindu Co-worker who looks upon his handicap as the means by which he has been encouraged to seek 'the truth that lies within':

I can't imagine what a crucifixion really is. I cannot concentrate on bleeding wounds. My pain is nothing by comparison, but I know that I am called to strive beyond my own small sufferings. Pain and pleasure, like heat and cold, come from the world of the senses. They come and they go; they are transient. Quietly but persistently I am called beyond them all to be at peace in pleasure and in pain, in gain and in loss, and in success or failure. In that peace there is no sin, no more confusion for all things are seen, felt, experienced in the heart. Be strong, I tell my soul, and don't be moved by passing fears.

Never let anything so fill you with sorrow as to make you forget the joy of the risen Christ.

MOTHER TERESA

As a girl, Jacotte wanted to be a missionary, and for a time she did manage to work in Algeria, but while she was there she contracted a chronic disease of the pancreas caused by a form of tropical parasite. Doctors were unable to treat this unknown parasite satisfactorily and so the illness recurred at intervals throughout her life. While she was in reasonable health Jacotte herself worked in a medical institute, but during her ever-increasing bouts of sickness she suffered not only from terrible physical symptoms. Because of a fear of infection on the part of those around her, she knew too the sense of isolation, the loneliness which Mother Teresa has identified as the particular poverty of the West and the worst disease of all. In November 1976, while still in her forties, she agreed to become a Sick and Suffering Co-worker. Recognizing that the mere thought of the suffering poor had often helped her to regain courage and confidence, she wrote to Jacqueline de Decker:

1976 November 29

After receiving your letter I'm convinced that the good Lord is smiling at my joy. I already feel at one with you all and have discovered great happiness and the faith of a little child. It is all quite different now because I can find joy in all the loving care that flows from heaven to earth and back again. I have still been very tired this week but I kept reminding myself: 'I must watch over Sister Mary', and God gave me new strength.

1977 September

My Sister still has not written but she knows that I am with her in prayer. I am better but I have been officially classified as an invalid, totally incapable of continuing with my profession, so I am taking steps to carry on with a correspondence course in sociology. It gives me some degree of self-confidence on the material level. Inch' Allah.

1978 August

I have had amoebic dysentery for six months and on top of that have had an operation to remove all my teeth. But it's all right, the general infection has gone now and I have begun to walk again. I have just heard that Paul VI has died.

He loved the work of Mother Teresa.

1979 January

It is the time for New Year wishes so I wish you courage in the year ahead. I am trying to imagine my Sister at work. Here my illness continues to isolate me because, of course, people are afraid of catching it. I listen to the radio but I don't have many visitors from the local village. I try to keep in touch with former students at the Institute. I read and I knit and I certainly appreciate the warmth of my home in the winter. The parish priest brings me communion every month but I don't believe that my solitude is really filled in this way. I think that I should try and help others as much as possible but understandably my disease frightens people off.

When I was less doddery I used to run a group for handi-capped people which supported the work of a friend's dispensary, but at the moment I am waiting for the doctors to decide whether I have to go into a tropical institute where they could study the bug that keeps recurring in my pancreas. So let us keep our fingers crossed. There is a great deal that makes me laugh but sometimes I cry. If I ever get my strength back I hope to be able to relieve the pain of those who suffer.

March

A special greeting to my little missionary. I don't know where she is – in India I expect – but I try to be faithful to her.

I'm back in the hospital for some special treatment for my disease. I must admit that it's been hard. I had ten days of successive treatments and while I was still waiting for the results, I had a relapse. The amoeba somehow resisted all the antibiotics. It's been twenty-one years now. I can hardly believe that it is still there. But then it's had plenty of time to build a fortress for itself. The doctor tells me now that I must get my strength back completely before he can start treatment for the bug again. I am strong but as the years go by my courage is fraying at the edges. I am astonished that with so many immigrants about my bug still seems to be such an unknown entity. The powers that be have acknowledged that they simply don't know how to treat me.

To keep myself going I tell myself that this experience will help them to identify the disease and take better care of our immigrants. It is hard that the doctors make no progress, but hardest of all is the fact that my illness has driven my friends away. Now solitude is a terrible reality for me. Because of my exhaustion even my last correspondence link is slowly petering out. But at least here I have the care of the nursing staff – that's one piece of good luck – and when the fatigue is almost too great I remind myself that one of these days I shall make it to heaven.

May
They are talking about sending me to a well-known specialist in tropical diseases in Paris. I can't help trembling at the thought of a huge hospital, particularly as I already know that there is no miracle cure. My mother is another source of concern. If I were to go home and have an attack, I couldn't very well bang my head against the wall for her to see and hear. Though I try to keep my spirits up, I do cry. Sometimes it works; sometimes it doesn't. I do hope you have courage.

Ask God to grant me the means of making the task of those who help me easier. May I continue to hope that this disease will disappear and may I have the humility to accept whatever help is given me.

I still hope to recover. Now I see that joy helps us to live. I must tell you that I belong to a line of robust Alsace peasants. Still, I am placing all my trust in the link with my Missionary Sister and in God, who uses everything of mine to help her.

I think he is linked to all suffering in a very mysterious sharing. Yet I don't believe that the good Lord came into this world to have himself crucified. He came to us at Christmas in a state of complete trust, and I thank him for the blue sky, for medicines that alleviate pain and for caring doctors. They represent his radiant smile in our diseased and troubled lives. And I thank you too for continuing to share my path.

August
Can you tell my Sister that I am asking heaven to let me spend these days in communion with her – in her work, her prayer, her message of charity and of hope. It is hard to hold out alone but it does make me put the communion of saints into practice. More than twenty years of this bug. I would laugh, if only I could.

I had three months in hospital last time but am now back at home and am taking advantage of my current independence to do some housework and to rest. In the end the very solitude induced by my illness can become rest and peace.

One missionary coming back to be with his sick mother in this country was astonished at the loneliness of sick people in Europe. So, even if I accept the very human limitations of my own illness, I really must cry out on behalf of other invalids for the love and attention that brings so much joy.

I believe that my long illness has enabled me to share in the trials endured by millions of poor people. In heaven there will be no more pain and we shall all share eternal rest in God. Like the real poor, we sick must learn to place ourselves entirely in the hands of God, for God is the only wealth of the poor.

I don't fret too much for my Missionary of Charity Sister. The days go by quickly and her work is there in the thick of it. Jesus wants me to believe this and that I can help her with my nothing. That means I must believe in his care.

1981 February
The doctors here have given up trying to treat me. They don't have a specialist in parasitology, so I'm to go to a hospital in Lyons.

My professor told me that the damage done by parasites over so long a period cannot really be put right, but he is going to try and arrest their development and all things are possible to God.

I shall have a room to myself as I need to rest and in any case my particular physical trials are a trial to other people. It was actually fortunate that I was still here this morning because my mother fell over. Now I must have courage enough for two.

Of course, according to my mother, it's all my fault for going to Algeria twenty-five years ago. There, in Algeria, I sorted beans in a factory in one of the Moroccan slums and that's how I caught my wretched bug. My mother could not understand my desire to be a missionary amongst the poor, and my father said to me: 'You thought it was the will of heaven but perhaps it was just a dream, a whim. Whatever it was, it doesn't matter now. Keep it to yourself and try to get over it as best you can.' That was in 1958. He died thirteen years later with his rosary in his hand. But my mother simply can't forget that because of a mere 'whim' I can no longer do any social work at all. So now I must accept it all. As I'm not yet in heaven I must help her, and together we manage to live on my pension. People tell me that I should think of myself: 'Other people can do for her what you can't do', they say. So I told God: 'I have kept it all to myself for a long time but now I have to accept the poverty of no longer being able to keep quiet about my lack of strength, for my mother's sake.' And Jesus sent me a token of his loving care because he saw that this little flame was finally flickering. 'I, Jesus', he seemed to say, 'can still help you through your fellow man if my Father wills it.' At last everything seemed simple and I found peace. I'm reminded of that saying of Mother Teresa's: 'never let your heart be so filled with sorrow as to forget the joy of the risen Christ.'

Jacotte wrote to the Jesuit Fathers in Lyons to see whether she could establish a more direct contact with the Friends of Mother Teresa, but she was growing weaker. By April 1981 she weighed only 39 kilos, but still she continued to write:

I'm not gone yet. First of all the hospital didn't seem to be very keen to take me with my tropical disease and then my mother had the flu' and lost consciousness. Fortunately I was there at the time, so we both ended up in bed. I'm now due to go in on 25 April and I'm down in the dumps. How I dread the unknown! I would rather go to heaven and I've got to pack my bags. Inch' Allah. We shall see.

I've written to the Friends of Mother Teresa in Lyons so I shall know some of her family there. They have promised to visit me so I won't be totally alone and I shall have a telephone in my room. You see Christ has at last reached out his hands after so many months of solitude. As a prisoner I can't help wanting to escape – it's long, it's hard, but perhaps too, in a way, it will be marvellous.

My little Missionary Sister is in Australia so I am studying her country. She works with a smile, the smile of Christ who expects me to smile too.

June

Thank you for your message at Pentecost. I came back from Lyons ten days ago to pack another set of suitcases. I am to be admitted into a special institute in Haute Savoie. I would have preferred to forget about hospitals for a while. At Lyons, as Providence would have it, I was put in the care of a very good and kind specialist. I was tucked into bed immediately and after forty-eight hours the haemorrhaging stopped. After five weeks I was back in my chaise-longue because the tests for my bug showed negative, except in my blood. Patience.

I shall take my tape recorder to Haute Savoie to study Italian. Oh, to be able to dry my tears. To have the grace not to weep would mean to be in Paradise already.

The friends of Mother Teresa became my family for those weeks in Lyons. Some of them visited me every week and just the knock at the door was enough to cheer me up. I learnt from them some of the ways of Mother Teresa.

October
This morning I received your letter. Mine to you was waiting for someone to take it to the post in the village. All the better; I can answer straight away. Are there any Co-workers I could meet near here?

The doctors tell me to be patient . . . six months, a year, but why not dream a little and hope? I'm praying to God for his help. I think of your work and I pray for you too. Forgive me for not writing to my Sister. She knows that I pray for her but with the passage of time and no letters from her, it all becomes more 'abstract'.

1982 September
I've been at the seaside for a month – pine-groves, blue water, sand and sunlight on bougainvilleas. The sky and the sun are somehow providential. There are some wonderful blue days and starlit nights. I look well and I would love to go to the village and play the organ. I've even written myself down for a Bible study course.

1983 January
Tell my little Sister that I have been faithful to her. I have kept her only letter since 1977. I can picture her in my imagination and through prayer it all becomes real.

Suffering in itself does not bring joy, but Christ as seen in suffering does. We see Christ in two forms. We see him on the altar under the appearance of bread, and we see him in the slums, in the broken bodies of the forgotten people.

MOTHER TERESA

Mother Teresa encourages all those who work with her to centre their lives on the Eucharist for here Christ in the form of bread offers himself to sustain. Her vision is a simple one: 'How great is his love for us. He makes himself the Bread of Life to satisfy our hunger for love, and then he makes himself the hungry one — so that we can satisfy his love for us. Oh, the humility of God.' A Co-worker who uses part of her home as a collecting centre for sacks destined for India, provides a similar insight:

Many times I have ached all over through sorting and packing sacks for India, which has made me realize how hard the Sisters must work. This realization has given me the stimulus to work even harder, knowing that my meagre efforts are a part of their work and a saving grace for my poor soul.

Eleven of us attended a Thanksgiving Day. It was an interesting day but by late afternoon my jaw had had enough and the muscles went into spasm so that by evening I was quite drained with pain. It seemed to me that dear Jesus wished me to know that I must offer more. An experience I wish to share with you – during Mass I felt a strong, friendly, warm presence. It was so strong that it would seem it could be touched. It was good just to sit there and take in this 'company'. As Mass progressed a new understanding of the Eucharist became known to me. I was to know this – that the wafer *was* Jesus in all his humility, for us to take, just as it was. 'Know that this is me', or words to that effect, came to me and also the similar words, 'Know that I am with you'. There seemed too to be a sadness that we do not accept him in the plainness of the wafer – that we expect more and that we should understand that the Eucharist holds the passion, the agony of the crucifixion and his resurrection, that it is full of himself and his love for us. After Communion with him I did not experience that presence by my side, but felt so full of love for him that I felt fit to burst.

As for the meagre suffering of mine for my Sister in Patna – yes, I think I should like to continue. Pain is not always of a physical nature and it would be good for my soul to offer what the good God asks of me. I tremble at those words, but if my young Sister working so hard in Patna can offer her all, by the grace of God so shall I.

May God give us all openness to ways leading beyond our own selves.

MOTHER TERESA

A young Buddhist who is both blind and crippled insists that when his physical pain is at its worst he has the most extraordinarily beautiful interior experiences. In Christian terms they are, he says, 'a foretaste of the resurrection'. When asked to elaborate on his understanding of suffering, he dictated the following:

Suffering arises out of sin, in other words out of our being trapped inside ourselves and therefore experiencing the pain of our own limitations. If we surrender ourselves completely to God we do not suffer. The physical pain may well be there, even the mental pain, but in the depths of our soul we can be at peace. Pain is a physical reaction; suffering on the other hand, is due to conscious reflection on it. Self-centred human consciousness is the cause of the misery that is everywhere apparent in the world. Even primitive man suffered less than modern man because his powers of reflection were less developed and he lived more spontaneously in contact with the Source of all Being.

Jesus Christ on the cross went through the physical and mental agony which are the consequences of sin, but he submitted his soul to God and so redeemed the world. Pain and death became not the end but the means of entry into the divine life. Pain is only really evil when it is considered from the vantage point of the ego, from the vantage point of a self shut in on itself and so separated from God. When the self is surrendered to God, pain, even death, become merely a means of passage into eternal life.

All of us are called to sanctity because as Jesus himself said, we must be perfect 'like the Father', and in order to become saints we must suffer much for suffering begets life in the soul.

MOTHER TERESA

Through suffering a deeper level of awareness can be opened up, bringing with it a more profound perception of life and a sense of joyous serenity. In such serenity lies a form of healing, a healing that does not necessarily involve the restoration of some ideal of physical normality, the mending of broken bodies, but rather something more positive and more durable. True healing, it may be suggested, is progress and resurrection and is best understood in the contemplation of the wounds of the risen Christ which did not disappear altogether but which were instead glorified, transformed and somehow beautiful: 'Put your finger here and see my hands; and put out your hand, and place it in my side' (John 20.27). From Switzerland, Cella writes of a 'deeper penetration into the beauty of the world brought about by suffering':

I was born on a grey February morning in 1921, but the joy of my birth was marred somewhat by the fact that I was small and thin and weighed less than four lbs. I was baptized immediately. Outside it was bitterly cold and snow was falling on the ground. We had only one stove which was used both to warm the house and boil the kettle, and I was so small that I was put in a cheese mould and kept beside the stove for warmth. My eldest sister was my godmother and would have loved to nurse me but I was too delicate. Much to everyone's surprise, however, I put on weight. It was my mother who became progressively more unwell and after a while I had to be put into a home run by nuns who taught me to love God.

When, at the age of six, I was returned to my home, my mother was very sick indeed. My sister was too young to manage the house. My aunt helped us out but it was my father who had to work especially hard to feed and look after us all, and it was he who taught us how to pray and love God. Every day we would say the rosary together at my mother's bedside.

I was a quiet child, good at school but often melancholy. I cried a good deal except when in my father's company. Then one day my father took me on his knee and told me that Jesus loved my mother so much that he had called her to be with him in heaven where there would be no more pain for her. My father was very patient in answering all my questions about death and after the funeral he devoted himself entirely to us. He was so good, perhaps even too good, but he insisted that it was better to be a hundred times too good than to be just once not good enough. He went out each day at 6 a.m., eating his frugal breakfast on his way to work. It was a great privilege to have a father who could teach his children by example about the love of God and about courage in the face of adversity.

At the age of nine, I was taken seriously ill but I remember my father sitting on the end of my bed, holding my hand and calming my fears as I struggled against death. 'Smile at Jesus', he said, 'and your suffering will be more bearable', and I did it, just to please him.

At twelve I suffered another trial. Father was taken into hospital. He remained peaceful. 'God alone can help us', he told me. 'We must smile at Jesus.' And so I stifled my tears and my father was released from hospital, but he had a weak heart and he grew progressively weaker. Nevertheless, he managed to visit other sick and lonely people and sometimes I was allowed to accompany him. He taught me to see Jesus Christ in my neighbour. 'It is not important that we do exceptional deeds', he told me. 'But that we do them with great love. It is Jesus we visit and it is Jesus who acts in us. We are only instruments of God. We have to thank him that we can serve others. All the graces we receive come from our heavenly Father.'

When I was thirteen I had to spend several months in hospital with appendicitis. Each time my father left me after his daily visit I would cry, but my aunt told me that when I cried I broke my father's heart. She asked me to offer my pain for him. Eventually I was able to return home, but I remember vividly on 7 October 1975, the Feast of the Rosary, before leaving the house to go to Mass, I found my father praying so fervently before the statue of our Lady that I was deeply moved. That same evening, when I got home from school, I was told that my father had had a fatal heart attack. For me, it was terrible to see his inert body.

Despite the fact that everyone assured me that they wouldn't desert me, this was the beginning of a period of great loneliness for me. There were financial problems, problems concerning my guardianship and, above all, doubts. Why had God taken my father from me? Why could he not have taken me instead? For me this was the end of all security and affection, the end of all beauty in life. Where was God and his love? I could no longer smile at Jesus. I lost my appetite, grew very weak and began to cough. Eventually the doctor diagnosed TB, and so began an even more painful period of isolation. I had my own special plate and my own special glass and was removed from all contact with others, to prevent them from contracting my illness.

In a sanatorium I finally hurled in the face of a visiting priest all my anxieties and feelings of revolt. He listened to me without a word until I began to cough blood and was prevented from continuing. Then he bathed my face and calmed me with infinite gentleness: 'It's all right. It had to come out. It's only natural that you should struggle. God himself could not bear his heavy cross but he loved us and did it out of love. Be confident that even when the cross seems too heavy for your thin shoulders, God will give you the grace to carry it, if only you say as he did on the Mount of Olives: "Father, your will be done – not mine." There can be no Easter without the passion but Easter will come for you.' As he went on talking, slowly I became calmer. I asked to make my confession and after receiving the Sacrament, I felt comforted in the knowledge that I was reconciled with God. I never met this priest again. He died only a few months later.

In November 1935 I was put in a sanatorium in the Flemish speaking part of Belgium, but I didn't speak Flemish and I felt lost in the crowd of other children. I was like a wounded bird in a cold climate. It was a young Sister, who by answering my sad expression with an encouraging smile, conquered the heart of the orphan. She gave me a glimmer of hope and I began to accept discipline, to smile at others and to smile once more at Jesus.

It would take too long for me to recount all the next stages of my life: the moments of deep sadness and interior struggle, my release from the sanatorium, the sale of the family home and my separation from my brothers and sisters. Eventually, however, I was to return to the sanatorium to train to be a children's nurse and, by devoting myself entirely to the welfare of these sick infants, I rediscovered the sheer joy of living. God had not deserted me. Although my health was still precarious and I was easily exhausted, I was able to earn my living and was no longer humiliated. After some years I even became a supervisor.

At one time I considered becoming a nun but my love for children made me want to have a family of my own. It was during the Second World War that I met and married Marcel, a very devout man who shared my desire to build a home and family on Christian foundations. Marcel was twelve years older than me and so was something of a father figure as well as a husband. We were very happy together and soon I discovered that I was expecting a child, but I had to spend much of my pregnancy resting to protect it. Still, on 28 February 1949, after hours of anxiety I gave birth to a little girl, called Maggy. All our troubles were over – or so we thought; but then on 18 March our baby had a fit of convulsions and died. The suffering that accompanied that little girl's birth was blessed but the agony of her death was very different. We could not help wondering why God had given a life only to take it back again so very soon.

My husband comforted me with unlimited patience, insisting that we must remain open to God's love. Soon I was pregnant again and this time I remained in bed for the entire duration of my pregnancy. If we waited with apprehension, we did so with love also. I had time as I lay in my bed to pray a great deal, and when finally our second daughter, Amy, was born she was a beautiful, healthy child. When, however, I was able to leave the hospital and take Amy home I discovered that my husband had been suffering from an ulcer for some months. In time he recovered and it was he who looked after our daughter because no matter how much I willed myself to be strong, I seemed unable to recuperate. I reproached myself constantly for being unable to care for my family as a good mother and wife, and eventually the doctors informed me that there was something wrong with my 'nerves'.

One day I tried to get out of bed and fell over instantly in a faint. Finding that I was increasingly less able to stand upright, I began to lose all confidence in prayer. I tried to be cheerful for the sake of my husband and daughter but I did not want to live, if living meant total inactivity and dependence.

Then, in 1960, a friend offered to take me on pilgrimage to Lourdes. I yearned to be fully cured but I prayed only for the grace to live in dignity with my illness. I remember a blind girl in the same compartment on the train journey, telling me that Lourdes was a message of love and joy in accepted suffering, and yes, in Lourdes somehow I did learn to accept. I came back with a new confidence that I could live with my illness.

After a while I found myself back in hospital, this time with a broken hip, and later it was confirmed that I had multiple sclerosis. I was confined to a wheelchair. Learning to live with a handicap is a long and a hard school. Sometimes my hopes of recovery would soar, only to be dashed again; sometimes I could accept and sometimes I would despair utterly – and in all this my only consolation was a caring husband and a kind and wonderful daughter.

Suddenly one day I developed severe cramps and lost the use of my right hand. For a while too, I could not speak any more and then I found myself unable to pray. I felt totally lost again, especially since I could see the tears welling in my husband's and daughter's eyes. I could no longer bear a life that caused them such sorrow and I made plans to end it. By chance there was a bottle of sleeping tablets just within my reach and so the real struggle began: 'Don't do it for the sake of those who love you.' 'Do it because it is unbearable for them to watch you suffering in this way.' I had never imagined that it could be so difficult to resolve to commit suicide, but eventually my mind was made up. I was about to put the tablets in water when my gaze fell upon a crucifix hanging on the wall. The crucified Christ wore an expression of such sadness. Terrified, I flung the tablets as far away from me as I could. The bottle broke as it fell and I was left feeling ashamed and full of remorse.

Two weeks later I recovered my speech and was able to make my confession. I never did recover the use of my right hand but I rediscovered peace, serenity and God. Even though I had yet more protracted spells in hospital and another operation on my hip, I found to my surprise that I could accept my handicap with relative ease. I found too that I was able to do things with my left hand and, above all, that I could be an instrument of God's love. I remembered everything that my father had taught me about my being created by God and capable of use in his work of redemption.

The Link for Sick and Suffering Co-workers showed me that I could love the destitute of the world, the poorest of the poor, my brethren in Jesus Christ. Now I have one desire only: to accept everything God sends me in his love, in total serenity and abandonment. Now my sickness and disability has ceased to be an obstacle to happiness. I am at ease, more patient, more serene and so, even when I am beset by pain or difficulties, I find them much more bearable. I have discovered an enduring joy and have found that I can share that joy with others.

When we abide in the passion of Jesus Christ we penetrate more deeply into the beauty of the world, into his love for humanity, we understand better his desire to see us saved and happy. Yet what use is a kind word without a willing ear to listen? So, not only should we be ready to accept the love, the joy of God, but we sick people should express our joy when a visitor comes and thus give that person the happiness of knowing that their love also has been accepted. Happiness is in both giving and in receiving or accepting.

Many people seek happiness in pleasure, prosperity, power or glory. They cannot accept or understand that an incurable or a severely handicapped person can experience intense inner happiness despite his suffering. To them it is an

78

impossible paradox. Yet, after all my trials, my interminable illness and my spiritual rebellion, I now believe that I have a far better understanding of true happiness. I have had so much time to think and to discover the beauty of creation, of nature, of faith and of my neighbour. I have sought and found Jesus Christ everywhere, even in sorrow, poverty and despair, and the finding has brought me even greater joy.

A sick person feels differently from a healthy one – he feels small, helpless, lost in time. He can dream and meditate and contemplate God in his works of love, in the power of the universe, in plants and flowers, in animals and in man. Every act of creation is a work of love and what a joy it is to be able really to see the fruits of that huge explosion of love and feel that we are God's!

We must deepen our life of love, prayer and sacrifice, for compassion, love and understanding have to grow from within and from our union with Christ.

MOTHER TERESA

The message of a woman who has been ill for most of her life is that, though healing may come, it does not necessarily manifest itself in the way expected. Her experience, she recognizes, is not unlike that of St Paul whose physical symptoms were a means of healing his pride: 'And to keep me from being too elated by the abundance of revelations, a thorn was given me in the flesh, a messenger of Satan, to harass me, to keep me from being too elated. Three times I besought the Lord about this, that it should leave me; but he said to me, "My grace is sufficient for you, for my power is made perfect in weakness" ' (2 Corinthians 12.7–9).

Like St John, the writer proclaims that 'the truth will make you free' (John 8.32). Man is liberated through understanding, wisdom and the cessation of desire:

No doubt I shall only be able to explain very inadequately how it is that up till now my life has been rich both in hardships and in joys.

I am sixty, the seventh in a family of thirteen children and a sufferer from a hereditary illness which eventually causes extensive paralysis. I was more or less normal until I was ten but I haven't been able to walk for the last thirty years. The most difficult time was when I was about twenty. How I envied friends of the same age! How I longed to have their energy, their strength, to be able to run, ride a bicycle and carry sacks of corn as they did. They had the good fortune to be healthy. Why hadn't I been so lucky? Less agile and weaker than the others, I became the object of their mockery, which inevitably hurt me greatly. There were times when I wanted to die. Death seemed sweet to me and the thought that one day I would end up in a wheelchair became my Calvary.

I had an aunt and an uncle with the same disease. He was always joking and even managed to laugh at his handicap. It seemed quite incomprehensible to me at that time. I remember one day when I was still a child he said to a young girl: 'Would you like to change places with me?' (He meant that he would then be healthy and she would be an invalid.) 'Oh no', she replied. 'Well, I wouldn't like to swop with you either . . . ', was his response. That was too much for me. I didn't understand him. I couldn't understand him. I wanted to get better. I would pray as much as was necessary to make me whole. After all, didn't Christ say, 'Ask and you will receive'? I hadn't really understood what this meant, so I prayed for days on end. They told me that the cross we are required to bear never exceeds our strength. But this was too much. I couldn't, I wouldn't take it.

I ought to tell you that I have two brothers and two sisters with the same disease – which made my own hardships even more difficult to endure. I kept thinking of the two who were younger than me, who were destined to go through the same agony. I still have very painful memories of going to visit a specialist who had to certify that we were all three suffering from this same dreadful disease. Somehow one kept hoping despite everything, but afterwards there was nothing but anxiety in the face of a shattered future.

One day one of my brothers left us to get married. He was the one who always used to get me up in the morning. On his last morning he said to me, 'I shan't be able to get you up any more!' and I couldn't so much as answer him. It was all that I could do to stop myself from bursting into tears. That day I learnt how heartbreaking some separations can be. I had once seen one of my aunts weep for ages because her son had gone away, but I hadn't understood her suffering. 'She doesn't have to make all that much fuss', I had thought to myself. There again, I hadn't understood.

But God often leads us along unexpected paths and the hand that smites us is also the one that consoles. Gradually I began to accept my trials. I asked God for good health. I wasn't healed but he gave me his grace and joy and I discovered the joy of living. Suffering is a wonderful school. The most important truth that misfortune accepted teaches us is that sacrifice brings to man incomparable joys. But our lack of humility, our refusal to make ourselves available often prevents us from understanding the importance of the sacred in life. I have to admit that it has taken me twenty-five years to accept my handicap. I was lucky to encounter Christ en route.

Should one really speak of joy to those who suffer? Yes, because a Christian has absolutely no right to be really miserable. 'I give you my joy', said our Lord. And I can't help thinking of something an uncle of mine used to say: 'A Christian should always be singing'. If I have found the joy of living I owe it to faith in God strongly founded on Christ whom I receive almost every day, and on prayer which is the most powerful source of energy.

For me religion must take pride of place in the scale of values. Christianity is rich enough to make life thrilling. I think that I found the rightful place of suffering in my Christian life on the day when I *accepted* my handicap, but it was a long and winding road, which I believe must go on and on . . .

Suffering can be an evil, a painful evil. God did not want it and only Jesus Christ made of it a means of sanctification. And yet it remains a mystery, for suffering is not defeat or mutilation, but a victory. Once accepted, it helped me to discover the deep meaning of life. For many it is a means to a kind of natural and supernatural blossoming. How many sick people have admitted that their life is more wonderful because suffering has made it more fruitful. Suffering need not therefore be evil, for evil is everything that prevents us from reaching our goal which is heaven! It is only in heaven that we shall really understand the value of suffering. The suffering of this life is only momentary but it tips an eternal balance of glory. It is a gift so precious that we should not exchange it for all the world. It is a means of expiation and it is better to undertake a thousand years of expiation on earth than a single hour in purgatory.

Yes, for me it is a precious gift. My condition allows me time to live, read, pray, think and seek God, for to seek God is to seek happiness, to find God is to find happiness, and to give God through my own weakness is to give happiness. A former invalid once told me: 'There are moments when I miss my time as an invalid. Now that I'm working my life seems quite mad!'

Truths on which we have meditated a hundred times are suddenly illuminated – the cross, a blessing! The idea may seem extraordinary to many. Yet the sign of Christianity is the cross. When the priest baptizes us he makes the sign of the cross; when he blesses a marriage again he makes the sign of the cross and he wishes the newly-weds happiness.

The world is full of crucifixions. This life is the way of the cross. The cross is unavoidable and indispensable, for would life be possible at all without discomfort and sacrifice? Our world is fraught with so many crises. Isn't this because we have lost the spirit of what is sacred, the spirit of the cross?

Be not afraid. God loves you and wants us to love one another as he loves us. As miserable, weak and sinful as we are, he loves us with an infinitely faithful love.

MOTHER TERESA

Like so many others, this Sick and Suffering Co-worker from France first heard about the Link through one of the numerous books on Mother Teresa's work. Her understanding of it is of a circle of spiritual bodyguards whose role is to protect those engaged in active missionary work, and with an irrepressible sense of humour she refers to herself as Jacqueline de Decker's 'Gorille', a play on the French word's dual meaning as both a personal bodyguard and a gorilla.

Sadly, she waited to no avail for a letter from the Sister with whom she was actually linked, but her letters to Jacqueline form almost a diary of her hopes and fears, her anguish and her joys. They also bear out the truth of the words of another suffering Co-worker: 'Often it is the sick who understand each other best. Sometimes it takes wounds to heal wounds.'

1974 March 27
As a handicapped person in an old people's home, I frequently come up against death, so the need to give value to life is all the greater. Before I was sick, I was a nurse in a children's hospital so I would like to adopt a Sister who

works with children. I am already praying for her in advance and derive great joy from my prayers for I believe in the communion of saints and spiritual support between brothers and sisters.

June
Please write in large letters with a big, fat pencil because my eyesight is bad and I can only write with a guide. This adoption has brought me great joy – you simply can't imagine how it has brought meaning into my life. Something has changed dramatically.

1975 May
At Lourdes I thought about my adopted Sister N. At Lourdes, one feels small, lost in the crowd but at the same time one really has a sensation of belonging to the Church.

1976 March
If I had been healthy I would have been a missionary but I know there is no way out of this illness which grips me. Several months ago a change took place which necessitated radiation treatment. The illness was arrested but the harm is done. It caused a metastasis – so now submission to providence, surrender, oblation must go hand in hand with calmness, rest and a restricted life.

November
You know that every important person has one or more bodyguards to protect him, so may I be your little bodyguard through prayer and offering? (You, after all, are Mother Teresa's bodyguard.) Then I'll plead your cause before heaven and the world.

I am undergoing deep ray treatment and it's tiring, but what is even more tiring is the smiling mask that I have to put on so that my mother doesn't worry. Still I live each moment to the full with love, enthusiasm and humour. Here I knit for Mother Teresa, carefully following the pattern you sent me and I'm also involved in the library for the home.

Every day I place my heart and my head at the disposal of the Lord – my eyes so that some priest in danger may find the light, my arms and hands for you so that you can continue your wonderful task as International Link for the Sick and Suffering, and my legs so that Mother Teresa can walk. She is so much in need of those legs. Only a short time after I offered my hands for you I had a very painful attack of arthritis in my shoulders and in my fingers. You'll appreciate that that attack filled me with joy because it meant that the Lord had accepted my suffering. I lay your poor hand and your stiff, immobile finger in the hand of Christ in the manger, and a current of love flows and is intensified through the joining of those hands.

December

In my case illness didn't steal upon me like a thief in the night. It simply appeared quite openly as my companion at a very early age . . . But no one quite knew what it was . . . It has only just shown its true face: CANCER. The name alone is enough to make you shiver. I wrestled, just as Jacob wrestled all night with God. Rebellion raged, and raged for a very long time indeed. It was only the movement 'Cœurs Vaillants – Âmes Vaillantes' that restored my zest for living. It made me feel that I wasn't a complete 'good for nothing' after all, since I was entrusted with the care of some sick and handicapped children. In that way I actually had to LIVE what I told them, which was to 'keep smiling', and I am still living by that slogan today.

Going into hospital is a hard school . . . You are case No. 24 or file No. 15, etc. If you're the big white chief's case then you have the right to a visit to the amphitheatre and the right to be the subject of debate but you have no apparent right to know anything. 'What's wrong with me? What are they going to do with me?' I kept on asking and when I did find out I had to change course completely and put everything in its rightful perspective.

I have always been drawn to the missions. Even though I

was unable to marry, I still have 'my' children. Pierre, Roger, Jean, 'my' priests in Africa, 'my' little lepers, my goddaughter Sister N., one of Mother Teresa's girls in the Indies and a Carmelite House in Madagascar. They all help me to forget my horrible illness and find JOY. At night, for example, when the effect of the sleeping tablets wears off too quickly, the pain often keeps me awake. So, without any real regard for time differences, I go off on an outing to visit 'my' children and with them I make my offering and pray. After Pierre, Roger and Jean, its 'my' little lepers' turn: What are they doing? And what about those other little mites who are so very hungry? I spend some time with them, with their parents and with the Sisters who look after them and give them their lessons. Then I set off for India to find my Missionary of Charity Sister and Mother Teresa. Finally, I go to adore the host in the Carmelite house in Malgache where Jesus waits for me in silence. Suffering . . . prayer . . . a kind of messenger service . . . mine are modest gifts (but there I must tread carefully – just so long as I have the strength and ability to pray and to suffer no matter how modestly). Am I unhappy? Not me, for I have found true joy. Every morning I receive my Lord . . . and every night I 'meet' my children. What more could I ask? And so with each new day it's just a case of 'keeping on smiling'.

1977 January 2
My knees are swollen and painful. I am waiting for my quack. Is it a metastasis or arthritis? Either way, it is just so that Mother Teresa can walk. Be joyful. God is everything. He is our heavenly Father. He loves us and we are in his hands.

January 9
Mother Teresa obviously has a lot of walking to do because on Monday I have to go into the clinic for an operation on my leg. I am pleased that the good Lord took me at my word. My joy is great – but oh, I'm no superman. I suffer

and I wish that the suffering were over, even though there is a spiritual joy in it.

January 23

Your letters make me very happy. It's just as if you come to visit me. Nobody actually says anything but I think that the cancer has taken a turn round my knee. Still if God can only relieve Mother Teresa of her exhaustion as she does her rounds, it's all worthwhile.

Mother Teresa, that tiny little woman – what a great woman she is! There can never be too many of us to help her to continue. I am tired but may my tiredness alleviate hers. I'll stop now.

January 24

I am calm and in a state of surrender . . . yet staggered to see how close God is and how he takes us at our word, and to what extent he expects our fidelity. This evening I am weary, empty headed . . . but this morning I received Jesus. He is my strength.

January 30

I am sleeping badly and in my thoughts I am undertaking quite a lot of missionary journeys to Madagascar and India, sowing the seeds of prayer. And I think a great deal about heaven. Do you realize what is waiting for us? . . . We shall actually see God as he really is and we shall be like him! . . . We the bandy-legged cripples of this world, with our dark glasses and our backs all twisted with suffering – there we shall be without our afflictions . . . all that will be behind us, so take heart!

February 4

What riches I have to place at the disposal of Mother Teresa in order that her wonderful work may grow and spread throughout the world . . . for what a treasure store suffering is. You know, sometimes I'm afraid of what the Lord dumps in my lap and I make very poor use of it because at times (though not all that often) I do hear the rumblings of revolt, and every now and then my offering lacks vigour. Still, now that I am your little 'gorilla bodyguard' less is lost. I carry you but I sense too that you are carrying me. You see, the more the eyes close to exterior things because the eyesight is softly fading, the more the eyes of the soul open and the more I find everything beautiful. As for my legs, since I've had such a long taste of bed, I bless them just for supporting me when they can . . . my hands are all right but cancer lurks below my waist and in my skull so it's better not to mention those areas . . . The growths in my back and knee are painful and give me trouble but they are, after all, only the small change given in payment for something so very valuable, so I still love them and that enables me to be your little gorilla bodyguard, so all's well!

You've seen my photograph – not a pretty sight with all that eczema on my face. I need my teeth replacing just to stop my nose from meeting my chin. Nature didn't intend them to be quite like that!

I'm sending you my little prayer book – it's truly marvellous . . . we shall see the bridegroom, because even I in all my glory am his 'bride to be'. At last to see him in his true splendour and love – what a prospect, what a day that will be! And since we read in the Gospels that he has a special predilection for cripples . . . yes, that's some promise. It helps one to carry on living.

It's true that when the scales are empty and we don't move they remain perfectly in balance; it's only when we start wanting to do things for ourselves that the balance is disturbed – one should just hand everything over to God.

I'm feeling bad. I'm going to lie down and offer myself. That's the essence of real friendship – one can build a bonfire of love out of anything.

February 17

You must come and go while my role is behind the scenes. As a secret, silent worker, I pray and offer what I can. I'm going to take a tonic and so intensify my prayer to be better able to play my role, as your 'bodyguard'. You're part of a charismatic group? There isn't one here but there is a spiritual centre where I go to pray. There I find calm, peace, silence and the opportunity for prolonged, private prayer. Those are intense times.

March 5
You feel that you are poor because your operations drive you into a corner. It's in those very corners that we are made to recognize our limitations and yet it's when we are cramped and wretched that the Lord is near. I am linking my own suffering to yours. With you I am poor, I suffer, I love and I try to smile and face the day that is the Lord's.

March 13
How are you and how's your arm? I simply can't wait to hear. Things are ticking over here; the radiation treatment's finished – thank goodness. If you only knew how empty I am. I haven't an idea in my head and yet I have so many things to tell you – poor old brain! But you'll understand. Between companions in suffering there is a wordless understanding because the experiences are really lived.

March 22
I love the Feast of the Annunciation, the day when the Virgin Mary said 'Yes'. On that day Christ, humanly speaking, was at his smallest and therefore very close to us. This is a part of the Christian mystery that I particularly love and for me it calls to mind so many 'Yeses' to God, particularly my promise to offer up my sufferings.

April 11
Apparently I'm not generous enough. That will have to change. I am praying hard that the Lord will give you back the use of your hand.

Together let us lift up our hands in a gesture of complete offering but also in a gesture of expectation of divine aid. Hands open, eyes closed – what a beautiful attitude of prayer. Easter follows Good Friday – that's the good news. I am praying to God the Father (in fact he is even more; he is a mother too) for he alone can grant us the necessary patience.

May 25
I have been to Lourdes and how happy I was there! It's strange how one can be very tired, exhausted even, but somehow happy. We spent long hours at prayer. We thrilled to the splendid and truly ecumenical ceremonies at the Basilica of Pius X. We were like one big, happy family and I dipped your hand with mine into the pool in order that you might be able to continue to face everything that your daily work involves. Again I am having deep ray treatment for my knees and back, but the doctors still want to avoid those dreadful mutilating operations.

From the standpoint of my faith I have a certain respect for this illness and the general state of things. That's not to say I like it, but at least it is useful for others. Nature could well do without it because it hurts – very much. I have had no news of my Sister.

August 15
I always enjoy the review *Amour sans Frontières* produced in France. Reading about Mother Teresa has really transformed my life. When you look at her you simply can't remain just ordinary. Here the old nuns are not very open to life today. There is uneasiness among the young Sisters because the Superiors are very authoritarian and so there are no more novices or postulants.

August 21
Mother prays faithfully for her Sister Francie but what a trial it is that it was Sister Frances who actually received the letter. All those names must make the correspondence very complicated. I have to admit that at the moment I am praying very poorly; and on top of that, something has cracked in my head. It's as if I am split in two. I go about like a sleepwalker. This must be spiritual gold but I am not generous – I am only a rough and ready bodyguard who is not fulfilling her function very well. I promise to take

myself in hand because you're not being properly guarded. I shall pray hard before I go to sleep and offer up my pains.

October 7
What joy your letter brought me at the thought of your happy hours spent among the Co-worker Links in London. You know, I am so close to you that my silence isn't really one at all; it's a close union of souls.

October 8
It's the middle of the night and my mother is asleep so I'm keeping very quiet. Perhaps this night is hard for you too. Very carefully, so as not to wake you, I am coming to lay my stabbing pain on your bed. I am putting everything there, offering it to you for Mother Teresa, and for you whose useless bodyguard I am. The weather is bad and my back hurts, my knee cracks at the slightest movement. It is swollen and so painful I want to whine. Worst of all are the heart and stomach spasms that give me an intense stabbing pain. At times I don't know where to put myself and that makes me moan and groan. Yes, I'm in pain but nothing must be lost of these riches. Offer them up with me.

I go and lie down and set off for India to Mother Teresa and Sister N. From there I shoot off to Madagascar where I have two godchildren . . . then to Benin to find my seminarist who is preparing for his diaconate. Afterwards I return to India to a little orphan goddaughter, then on to Madagascar again to the Carmelite mission at Ambala, then it's back to you and afterwards the sheer exhaustion of all that travelling brings me sleep for then my heart is happy. That's what a night of real missionary work consists of.

How is that poor hand of yours that you need so much? I am reading the Acts of the Apostles straight through from beginning to end. They are tremendous. I'm discovering the power and might of action of the Holy Spirit. The apostles have such audacity. What extraordinary lessons there are to be learnt from them. What a good thing it is that Mother Teresa created the Link for the Sick and Suffering, the bodyguards. It gives us wretches a real sense of usefulness because it's impossible just to keep doddering on when we know that the Sisters can only carry out their work if we do ours!

I am sending you a whole load of things via the guardian angels: terrible tiredness, a violent stomach-ache that preys relentlessly on the nerves and a 'growth' which is reforming itself below my knee – there's the shield that my affection is providing for you. May God be your strength and your support.

November 1

It's All Saints Day, a festival I love because I believe whole-heartedly in the communion of saints. For me it is a powerful union of all those here below with those who are with God. Above all, it's the festival of all those for whom I have a special affection.

Often I visit you in thought and throw off my back-pack. 'Here you are, Lord, this is for Jacqueline', I say, 'so she can have a healthy back!'

There are so many things to pray for. You know, for some time now I have prayed in the mornings that I may allow Christ to speak to his Father through me. That changes everything. Prayer becomes praise and like St Paul I can say: 'And I live now not I, but Christ who lives in me.' I disappear and that can't be bad, can it?

November 18

The 21st is the day of the Presentation in the Temple, another feast day that I love because it commemorates a pledge.

I am like you. For great causes and ends I'll give my everything, but small ones exasperate me and I get niggly. So, as from today I'm going to make more of an effort because you must be able to get about – you must be able to stay upright and strong; I in my old people's home (even though I'm only 54 years old) shouldn't just give up and relax. I'm limping because of my knee but even if I were to have another operation on it, it would only be my eighth, whereas you hold all the records.

November 20
I'm back again because I missed the post and I'm adding this thought for you: 'I am more conscious each day that even if the earth itself passes away, God's plan will endure. God has planned every instant for us. That means that we should give value to the present, live the present to the full in order to be good bodyguards for each other. It's not important for us to imitate, to ape the great saints but rather to fulfil God's plan for us lesser mortals, by helping each other even as we rely on God.

December 22
Take a look at this pretty picture of these two little gorillas side by side. Aren't we sweet? And see how united we are! Isn't this the portrait of our friendship? Thank you for the letter from Sister F. and its translation. My mother was delighted. She was very touched by the letter and prays fervently for her little Sister. This sentence of St Paul's. 'And the very God of peace sanctify you wholly; and I pray God your whole spirit and soul and body be preserved blameless unto the coming of our Lord Jesus Christ' (1 Thessalonians 5.23), is a good expression of my wishes for you in this liturgical year.

And now that orthopaedic collar of yours is playing you up! That's what happens when you want to hold your head up too high . . . joking apart, poor thing, it can't be very pleasant to be armed with such a contraption. How much help Mother Teresa must need, for you to have to be constantly on the rack like that! My thoughts and prayers are with you even when I don't write.

Here our two other Sick and Suffering Co-workers are growing old. With me things are just about ticking over. My heart beats too slowly, my back and knee keep me on a tight rein and every now and then a slight syncope reminds

93

me that I have to keep an eye on my ticker. My Sister N. still shows no sign of life . . . it would give me great pleasure to have one of those French Sisters in Haiti to adopt. How marvellous it is that all those youngsters are seeking to give themselves so totally and absolutely.

1978 January

Oh, dear friend, I feel for your confusion at the loss of the dear old uncle you looked after in your flat, but have no fear, he won't fail to give back a hundredfold those little acts of kindness that you gave him. May he obtain many graces for you and provide you with strength. He, after all, has found joy.

I too, have just turned over a page in my life. I have just had an attack of angina pectoris. From now on, I'm to live in slow motion. I shall offer this constraining bit of string round my paw for your activities and so be close to you. I'm stupid and I don't really know how to explain to you that with all my strength I am holding up in outstretched arms this crazy, lazy heart of mine. May this clumsy offering be your protection, a means of support in your life, so entirely devoted to Mother Teresa through the love of God.

February 2

Today I am bubbling over with joy. I am coming to you. I am on a six-day retreat at a spiritual centre (Chaillé). We had a marvellous service of penitence. I have never before experienced such joy in my soul. We cripples are God's chosen ones, his favourites, for Christ came for the sinners and the sick, and it is he who fills us to overflowing.

Yes, you see with this knee, this back and this ailing heart I am still experiencing profound joy. He has raised me up. I have sinned and I have been pardoned.

April 15

Today is the anniversary of my baptism, a day that I love. So your new corset isn't too good? Poor thing – Jesus must love you to accept your offering for Mother Teresa in the way that he does. Tomorrow I shall take you with me to Lourdes, I shall involve you in everything: prayer, offering, tiredness, absolutely everything!

Easter

I too recognize myself to be a sinner and poor like you and with you and you're right to say: 'God is our wealth'. I used to have a little goddaughter in India, an abandoned child in Tamil Nadu. She went to heaven on the day of my operation last year. She was nine months old and had been baptized one month previously. The Sisters sent me a photograph of her. Now every evening that little Miriam acts as my messenger and I send her to the Lord, bearing my prayers for India.

Knitting is one thing I can still cope with. Tell me where I can send a parcel of woollen children's clothes. It would give me such pleasure to think that one of those children suffering from the cold might be warmed. I assure you that they are made with tender, loving care. I still have your vest patterns and have actually managed to make some.

May 6

Life goes on after my pilgrimage to Lourdes, but this year I have discovered to exactly what extent I am restricted. FIAT. Every evening I play a little music. It relaxes me and leads softly into prayer. For me prayer is really a heart-to-heart with the Lord and I love this time of the evening because it is now I learn to love him more.

June 3

I have just had a bad attack of arthritis. I had a hard time of it. In fact, I felt just as if I'd swallowed a broom. But now it's easing up. I've had to go back to the radiation treatment too, and I'm still very tired. Everything seems to set my nerves on edge.

August 6

Our exchange of letters is such a source of joy. In October

there is a Charismatic Renewal meeting and the thirst for prayer consumes me. It is quite a discipline to impose half, three-quarters or maybe even an hour of prayer on oneself in total silence.

August 29

You have been suffering spiritually but as you do so much to help the Sick and Suffering Co-workers to accept their suffering and offer it up for the Sisters, you really shouldn't take on material tasks. You'll have to change your attitude a little – to fall in with obedience, no matter what it costs, and then you will be transfigured anew and you will be sure of making no mistakes. Place your submissive 'Yes' in his hands and God will show you his will for you. I'm saying 'Yes' with you. Rest assured of my affection and my prayers.

September

Hello, friend, friendship makes us so close, doesn't it? You know, the more you think about it, the more you realize that God asks us to renounce ourselves. Mother Teresa too asks detachment of us. We must ask God what is to be done for all those souls who take the cause of the poorest so well in hand. Have confidence. 'Give them through our hands this day their daily bread.' Your prayer will be answered in the mystery of faith.

Let us allow ourselves to be jolted every now and then – sometimes we think that we are concentrating on the essentials when really we are passing them by. Let us put everything in the hands of the Lord and peace will gradually come. Take St Joseph in the Gospel. He thought he was doing the right thing and the angel spoke to him and he understood everything.

Did you see those disasters in India? What terrible suffering there is there! I am offering myself for Mother Teresa. May the Lord keep her, grant her light and sustain her too.

I think it's great that the name they have given your illness is the 'SS disease'. You are incurable and so am I.

I'm back with my radiography, tests and radiation treatment. The two of us put together wouldn't make up a whole and healthy woman. And both our medics have decided on next week. Amen. In heaven we shall see the meaning of our suffering. Meanwhile let's make good use of it. It is so powerful. Goodnight . . . it is so peaceful when everyone's asleep.

October 29

You've had a spell in the clinic for examination. That really is a form of martyrdom and one is more tired afterwards than before. They issue endless orders: give blood, blow in there, look over here, allow yourself to be photographed in the nude, then afterwards they have the cheek to tell you that considering all that's wrong with you, you're in quite good shape! You certainly need a sense of humour.

1979 January 6

Epiphany. I'm coming to talk to you even though your little gorilla bodyguard can hardly think straight. Do I have to continue writing to my little Missionary of Charity Sister? There is still not a peep out of her despite the abundance of Christmas mail you mentioned. What about you? How are you? Are they still chiselling away at your back, your hand, your teeth and your orthopaedic collar. I ask you is it reasonable, all that? As for me, I'm trying to come to terms with my old carcase. My heart is very slow again (44 to 46), and my left arm hurts but my morale is good.

May 8

Your little gorilla isn't very chatty at the moment. Often I haven't the strength to face up to the menu for the day. My mother has not been well. Her faculties are slowly failing her. Everything is becoming a problem for her, but we pray together for the Missionaries of Charity, for you, for everyone.

September 15

Your note has arrived and I was greatly touched by it. It all happened so quickly. Mother and I went for a short walk. In the evening we prayed together and the following day we found her motionless, with staring eyes. She'd had a cerebral haemorrhage. Next day at noon we caught her last breath.

Certainly the hope is great but so too is the sense of separation, especially for me because I lived constantly in her company. It will take time for the wounds to heal. It's at such times that one senses the support of the family and friends, but in my heart all is pain, and in my body too.

I'm doing my best to listen to the pensioners in the home with all their tales of woe – crushed hearts, breathless hearts who tell the same tales one hundred and one times over. I am showing them how to pray with open hands, in the way which offers everything and expects everything.

1980 January 3

There has been a gap for a while but only in our correspondence because, knowing you to be very busy, I have been close to you. Since the decease of my mother I have had to reorganize my flat. My brother comes round every now and then. Otherwise life goes on as before. The hospital examinations weren't too wonderful. Fortunately I look all right so they leave me in peace. The King's secret is well kept.

February 12

My wishes are for peace, joy, light, health and holiness. Here my ministry is still to listen to the grannies and grandpas. I often speak of you to the Lord. Mother has spent her first Christmas with God. She must be progressing from one marvel to the next. Everything must be so different up there from how our human brains conceive it.

The emptiness of her absence is greater at festival times but I don't want to tarnish joy with tears, and I wish you health sufficient for you to face your daily work. As for me, I take longer to do my daily tasks now. Fortunately, to the Lord it is not the effectiveness that counts, but the effort and the heart put into the doing.

April 6

My heart often seeks out Mother Teresa. How we must support her, she is so simple and humble – how many lessons she teaches our poor world!

The sun floods my room; and the birds are singing their hearts out. The thought of soon going to Lourdes fills my heart with joy. You won't be forgotten there. Here there are still the same trials – pray for them.

July 28

You sent me news of Mother Teresa. She seems quite tireless and her work grows even greater. Let us pray for her. Here my heart beats slowly on. Life is very simple, divided up into prayer, knitting, rest, letter writing, service.

August 5

Tomorrow is the Transfiguration – let us be transfigured through the grace of Christ whom we receive in the Eucharist.

September 2

I have had to take a complete rest at the Convent of the Visitation and the Sisters took care of me, but I had a glandular attack with terrible pains for five or six days. The Lord sent me a fragment of his cross.

December 20

My shoulder is blocked. Therapy doesn't help. My wishes for you are the same every year: peace, serenity and joy.

1981

My news is becoming less frequent but I am faithful to you.

1982 March 7

The cardiologist is going to put a pacemaker in my heart – 42 beats a minute. It's tiring. Amen. On Good Friday I suffered a heavy moral blow and now my words are all mixed up. I try to say 'Yes' but to live it is difficult.

August 4

Sometimes my pulse drops to 40. Our charismatic group is growing. There are twenty-eight of us and the meetings are fruitful. They sustain us for the entire week of the received word.

1983 February 11

I had a very rich spiritual experience at the beginning of this year and that experience lives on in me. The soul's experiences of God are difficult to express. It was at the hospital while they were giving me my pacemaker and I was in the intensive care unit. I was aware of my smallness, of my weakness, of my wretchedness, but also of the infinite greatness of God, of his paternal love. Everything that our human eyes can't see down here – his radiance, beauty, light and majesty – we shall come face to face with it all in the end! I get by, just about, with this pacemaker. When it's working the motor moves my arm. It's certainly a most peculiar sensation to have a heart both on the left and on the right. I remain very restricted in what I can do and very tired, but I have my finger on the true value of life, the sheer greatness of life.

Happiness is the sign of a generous person. It is often the mantle of self-sacrifice. Joy is the surest way to announce Christianity to the world.

MOTHER TERESA

Remarkably, those whose strength is most heavily taxed are frequently those who are most ready to give of what little is left to them. In 1972 the writer of this letter lost the use of her legs in a car accident. She also has a son who was born handicapped, and for a while she suffered from such severe depression that she was unable to speak.

I am paralysed from my chest to my feet and so, dear Sister, all that I can offer you is a smile, which is sometimes spontaneous, but which often only thinly hides my suffering. I offer you also my silence, my bitterness, my anger and all my yearnings. I offer you my past, which was by no means exemplary. I offer you all the humiliation of being paraplegic and of needing constant help. I offer you everything I can't do, but I offer you also all the things that I can do, for I can still help blind people with my eyes and my writing. I can discover love for others through the love of God. I offer you also the care of my handicapped son. I know that I can have a joyous heart because I can lift up my eyes to look at those who are less fortunate than me. Now, after hiding within myself for so long, at last I can offer to God my mad desire to run through long grass and pick flowers, and I can find the courage to smile at Jesus.

There is a tremendous strength that is growing in the world through this continual sharing together, praying together, suffering together and working together.
                                        MOTHER TERESA

If suffering is a mystery permeated with sadness and joy then one of the most extraordinary and joyous aspects of it is the way in which those who suffer yearn to use their experiences to bring relief and help to other people. This first letter from a woman confined to a wheelchair with muscular dystrophy is characteristic of countless others.

This letter seems rather difficult to write, for how are we to get to know each other? How am I to start? I am thirty-four years old and live alone in a flat specially adapted for my electric wheelchair, which makes it possible for me to get about. I have some monthly financial support to rely on, and we have an intercom system which enables me to call for assistance whenever necessary. Thus on the material level I lead a rather comfortable life. Fortunately, however, I experience other forms of poverty, especially the poverty of sickness. I suffer from muscular dystrophy which will eventually induce total paralysis. But for the time being I am mobile and strong enough to undertake certain activities in the complex in which I live.

Nevertheless, sometimes I am worried by the way in which my physical strength is diminishing, and cling to what is left. I prefer to dream rather than to confront my personal reality. Yet the reality of love is within reach of everyone. It impels me beyond my human hopes and dreams. My life takes on new meaning and I look upon my sufferings in the light of the meaning of Jesus Christ.

The complex in which I live has 1,200 inmates, who suffer psychologically, physically and spiritually: broken families, battered wives, unloved children, drug addicts – the loneliness of old age, the burden of indifference . . . there are so many tearings of the heart of man. This complex is a microcosm of the world, a world to be loved, a world to be saved. It is this world which makes me really long for that great love which Jesus Christ has put in me.

And what if I were to tell you that I harbour another dream? That of being able to convey this love to all the bereaved, the destitute, those whose misery is so frightful that they barely qualify as human beings. Then I could become a missionary through my prayers and my offering for you and all those you touch, look at and care for. Then my being with its capacity for giving and surrender would bring strength to your hands, your heart, your tiredness and your presence amongst the poorest of the poor, while in the heart of this complex, where there is so much hidden suffering, I live on in faith and in the hope of seeing humanity grow more in accordance with God's plan of love for mankind.

United in Jesus in this way, love must be alive, and there

must be a strength which links us to the very extremities of the world.

We are neither big nor small but what we are in the eyes of God, and as long as we surrender ourselves totally then God can use us without consulting us. We like to be consulted but letting him use us without consultation is very good for us. We must accept emptiness, accept being broken to pieces, accept success or failure.

MOTHER TERESA

Almost all the Sick and Suffering express a sense of the smallness and inadequacy of what they can offer, yet there is unlimited hope to be derived from the knowledge that no action is too small for God, nor is any form or degree of suffering unacceptable. It is not the magnitude of the action or the severity of the pain which is important, but rather the love that is put into the offering.

A teacher 'tormented by interior battles' was delighted to discover that he could offer his minor day to day sufferings for Mother Teresa:

I was overjoyed to have a 'visible purpose' in prayer; but almost immediately God took it away and the sense of my own effort in praying and the hope of its result have mercifully been withdrawn. Now all I have to do is plod on without feeling or thinking anything, trying to remember to pray regularly for Mother's work among the poor and just keeping going, trying not to object to the usual ills and ailments one has offered one. It is good – I rejoice at this, that consciousness of my own effort has been removed from me.

What a great blessing! God can't do anything unless I am nothing; through no merit of mine either of effort or good will, he has taken away what was getting in the way. I never realized before how valuable it could be, sitting still in the mist, just doing nothing but 'living and partly living', waiting. God went down to the bottom of hell and back and he never complained, so what am I doing moaning about this, that or the other, eh?

After a breakdown and illness resulting from overwork, he was able to write:

God has now put me in such a beautiful place, where he is healing me wholly, that I feel a hundred miles away from that aching emptiness and that struggle to cling grimly on to sanity and conciousness of the goodness of God and what he was working within me. I would not *like* to have to undergo this again, but now I believe I could *welcome* it, as I have had the experience of realizing what suffering can do to extend the soul and its capacity to love, and to receive love. I feel the six months I had to cease work is worth more in my soul perhaps than all that I have done heretofore. The help of the example of the saints, and the consciousness of offering suffering as part of the activity of someone else (it didn't matter that I didn't know who, or how, or when or where), gave me almost a sense of exhilaration, rather like surf-riding. It helped me to begin to understand the purpose of the passion (which I am still *far* from understanding). It made a link through Christ's wounds to God, and turned the world topsy-turvy, so that pain became joy, and hate and grousing became love and thanksgiving. I am a great admirer of Lewis Carroll, who perceived this (I suppose) when he made Alice go through the looking glass to become the 'right way round', as it were.

My sufferings are just tiny ones, like the myriad glints in just one very small piece of mosaic, that I offer up to go in the chalice, into which Mother wants all her good actions poured. Love is the cement that binds us – all the bits of mosaic – together. My efforts are very feeble, and the odd thing is, I don't feel I can 'offer' anything at all . . . in fact, I am actually *receiving*. Is this then what loving is all about?

More and more I turn away from suffering – I think I was being somewhat martyristically pious (a besetting sin of mine which needs much praying for). I long to be 100% shiningly fit and healthy because this kind of happiness can be a force for good. Being quietly happy sheds a kind of contentment all around and is good to feel both inside when it is flowing through you and outside when someone else has it and lets it go so that it heals you. I now feel that my physical limitations are perhaps a good thing; they prevent me from wasted over-exertion which leads to increasing speed which usually leads to a big jam. In the end it did for me. It's quite nice to be 'officially' indolent; minor injuries simplify choices, and life is slower, sweeter and far less busy and complicated. My suffering then, has *genuinely* been transformed into joy, since it need no longer exist, it's up to me what attitude I choose to take. Such reasoning makes one see 'suffering' in quite a different light.

4

'The medicine that strengthens our humanity'

> Christ came into the world to put charity in its proper
> perspective.
>
> MOTHER TERESA

*It was a former leading lady at the London Hippodrome who
described the horrors of depression and the utter desolation of
widowhood following a happy marriage. She spoke of recurring intervals of dark demoralization and hopelessness,
aggravated by physical pain resulting from having been run
over by a car at the age of four, of times when she simply could
not stop crying and periods when all hell broke loose and
peace was achieved only by uttering the prayer of rebuke: 'In
the name of Our Lord Jesus Christ, I rebuke you spirit of
fear. Get out in the name of the Lord.' For a while she lived
with the thought of suicide, with pills constantly at her side,
and even now, some years after her husband's death, she
admits to not having recovered from the 'whole agony of being
alone'.*

*Inevitably there were the questions: 'Why did God do all
this? Why did he let me suffer in this way?' But she spoke,
too, of moments when she had experienced a profound sense of
being upheld: 'While my husband was still alive we went on
a working party to Italy and one day we were high up above
Lake Como and I was wandering alone among the fields.
Then something indescribable happened. I was suddenly in
the presence of such joy, beauty and brightness, something so
overpowering. When I came to, I was standing with tears
pouring down my face, saying, 'I want to make everyone
happy.' I wasn't much of a Christian then.*

*'Again during the six weeks when my husband was very
ill and everyone expected me to fall to pieces a most amazing
thing happened. I suppose, not I suppose, I know the Lord*

stood by me, upheld me, and I grew stronger and stronger. I was able to nurse him with the help of a night nurse until his very last breath, and then I was so at peace and happy for him. On the night of the funeral my whole world collapsed but the peace that accompanied his death was the most wonderful experience of my life.'

She also referred to friendships which had been a great source of comfort and support to her, and of other relationships through which she in her turn had been able to counsel and sustain, and in conclusion she supplied the answers to her own questions: 'I must learn to trust the Lord and put myself in his hands, learn to leave my fears and troubles at the foot of the cross. The joys have been given me to sustain me through my trials and the trials have enabled me to understand and comfort others.'

The message of one of the Brothers who refers to a life 'lived more fully through pain' is not dissimilar. Whatever experiences the individual may have of discomfort or sorrow may be turned towards a better understanding of the suffering of others:

The apostle Paul, in his letter to the Romans, tells us that we are the heirs of God, the co-heirs of Christ, sharing his sufferings so that we might also share his glory. This is really the clue to our problem: as each one of us is an individual and unique, we cannot fully share an experience of pain with anyone else when suffering even something as common as a headache, a toothache or a stomach-ache. You probably have had all these at some time in your life; we all have. We could describe each one of these to you vividly in words, sound and gesture. But even if we recalled your pain for you it would be your pain recalled for you and our pain recalled for us. Nevertheless, we come close enough to have some sharing and so some sympathy; though, the less experience in a particular field, the less easy it is to realize what another is going through. How can we who, up till now, have not suffered arthritis know the pain of those we know and love and often visit, who can hardly stand or move from a chair? How can we who are not blind sense the pain of blindness? Or the blanket of deafness; or the dead body weight of a paraplegic; or the mental anguish of lying in a hospital bed, separated from family and friends? The truth is that we cannot experience your particular pain. But there is that element in trying to share in which we can only say, 'I know pain', rather than, 'I know your pain'. And, therefore, it is important in the brotherhood of man that we all, being born into a world of pain, in some degree experience it too. Again, what extraordinary, different effects pain has on different people. It is one of those pondering points about pain that it exists at all; but it is also a perennial problem that some people can take it and others, apparently, can not.

For it is true that the crucible of suffering purifies and ennobles some people in such a way that the person, like Job himself, seems to hear the voice of God in the tempest and positively radiates peace, joy and life. While others seem to shrink and shrivel and grow daily more bitter. The Christian facing pain is facing it with Christ – that is easy to say; it is much less easy to live, but it means that this is not just stoic endurance; it is pain suffered, pain fought, it is pain accepted and, in a sense, it is pain defeated. The element of suffering, of course, is not removed, but the suffering of Christ, somehow, penetrates into a part of us and leads us to greater endurance. All the same, we are normally left with one or two questions – in fact, the same old questions: why should I suffer or why should they suffer? And certainly we can pursue ideas but answers are elusive and unsatisfactory.

It is only by concentrating on God, by experiencing him in Christ, in yourself, and continuing to live openly and closely to your own pain or to those who suffer, that some measure of knowledge comes. If you truly love God, the pain does not go away, but you live more fully and in a way which can only be experienced. There is a new dimension in

111

which the figure on the cross, through pain and death, grows glorious, joyous and intensely loving in the resurrection.

Make us worthy, Lord, to serve our fellow
men throughout the world who live and die
in poverty and hunger.

Give them, through our hands, this day their
daily bread; and by our understanding love,
give peace and joy.

Lord, make me a channel of Thy peace
that, where there is hatred, I may bring
love; that where there is wrong, I may
bring the spirit of forgiveness; that
where there is discord, I may bring
harmony; that, where there is error, I
may bring truth; that, where there is
doubt, I may bring faith; that, where
there is despair, I may bring hope; that,
where there are shadows, I may bring light;
that where there is sadness, I may bring joy.

Lord, grant that I may seek rather to
comfort than to be comforted, to understand than
to be understood; to love than to be loved; for
it is by forgetting self that one finds; it is
by forgiving that one is forgiven; it is by dying
that one awakens to eternal life.

THE CO-WORKERS' DAILY PRAYER

*It goes without saying that caring for the sick is not always
an uplifting experience. Mother Teresa's directive to 'give until
it hurts' applies as much to those who undertake to care as to
those who are actually suffering. When problems or difficulties
arise, her solution to these as to every other 'insoluble problem'
lies in prayer. It is through prayer and the opening of the heart that*

the loss of self and the necessary understanding are achieved, for through prayer it becomes possible to perceive the true nature of another's need and to become a channel for the greater love of God, even in the most difficult or repellent of situations. From the United States a Co-worker writes on the subject of compassion:

I don't know what has caused me to read so many articles lately on the subject of 'compassion', but I think we, as Co-workers, are faced with compassion when we are with the poor and the lonely and the dying. Compassion asks us to go where it hurts, to enter into places of pain, to share in brokenness, fear, confusion and anguish. Compassion challenges us to cry out with those in misery, to mourn with those who are lonely, to weep with those in tears. Compassion requires us to be weak with the weak, vulnerable with the vulnerable, and powerless with the powerless. Compassion means full immersion in the condition of being human. When we look at compassion in this way, it becomes clear that something more is involved than a general kindness.

Whether you are a Hindu, a Muslim or a Christian, how you live your live is the proof that you are fully his or not.

MOTHER TERESA

The ultimate test of faith must be the fruits of the Spirit (Matt. 7.16). Mother Teresa calls upon the sick to suffer with the smile that is the most effective way of proclaiming Christianity to the world, and for those who come in contact with suffering borne in this way, that very encounter frequently brings with it a sense of renewed hope and a deepened understanding of what is holy. 'Those who apparently have nothing have so much to give' is the consistent message of those who are prepared to receive. One former national Link, herself no stranger to suffering, speaks of innumerable lessons learnt, not least of them an understanding of endurance:

So many of those people who wrote to me while it was my privilege to be a Sick and Suffering Link knew about endurance and passing beyond it. They were so helpful to me because the heights they were scaling towards heaven gave me a sort of yardstick on endurance. They did not know this as one could tell from their letters that they felt themselves to be the least of sufferers. Put all their letters into a computer and one sentence would emerge: 'I only have so little to offer.' This would equate with some of the most painful conditions of health or long term incurable illness. That phrase, 'I only have', remains with me now to carry me through many a day of depression or fatigue and reminds me to shake myself and say, 'For goodness sake, take up the little cross you have to bear and be grateful it is not more!'

We will all be given much to bear – not too much, nothing beyond our endurance. Knowing this, it is perhaps true that if we bear it as a stoic with gritted teeth, however commendable that way may be, it is somewhat negative and we may break under the strain. Should we not admit rather that we are brought to our knees and complain to our Lord? We are not then cutting ourselves off from him. Great characters may become greater through suffering endured stoically, but most of us break. It is then that we enter into such despair and destitution that it is hard to find a loving God within us. So endurance is not enough. Suffering must be linked to humility and to hope, to love of oneself in an eternal sense and to an awareness of belonging to God. In this way no moment of pain, either physical or psychological, will ever be lost, for it will be part of God's eternal plan of redemption. I do not have to believe this, only to hope in it.

Another national Link speaks of how 'in the company of some of the sick one is made quietly and simply aware of a great unity with Jesus and his passion'. 'I came away feeling humbled and yet thrilled to be alive', insists one young Co-worker. Another talks of 'the love of the Holy Spirit shining through friends in an hour of need', another of 'the sustaining joy of corresponding with a fellow-Christian'. Yet another refers to the 'unconscious healing interaction of individual lives — that mysterious process which brings someone in need of help to your door at the very instant when you are feeling most in need of company, most useless and most irrelevant'. Finally there was the poignant reminder: 'Have you ever considered what humanity would be without suffering?'

The encounter with life in its bruised and broken forms can bring with it a glimpse of the miracle of love in those very same lives, and a sense of being privileged — perhaps even of being blessed — to see the seemingly broken who are mysteriously healed, the seeming sinner who is a saint and the seeming poor man who is rich in hitherto unimagined ways. Inevitably sadness, despair, bitterness, confusion, all the negative emotions of which mankind is capable, may congregate at the bedsides of the sick and the dying, but for some there remains the awareness that they have been brought there to witness the miracle of God's presence born anew in the hearts of those who suffer. The last word is that of a self-confessed agnostic:

I cannot love a divinity that lets creation suffer blindly and afraid. But then when I see suffering without pettiness or indignity, without a sense of failure or despair, when I see this extraordinary abandonment to love and the prospect of death turned into life, it is I who feel myself separated from some higher principle of unity and wholeness.

Before the magnitude of pain and the fullness of joy I find myself limitlessly helpless, empty and vain. Who then is really blind, suffering or poor? Inwardly I weep for others who do not really need or want my tears, and I weep most of all for myself. And when my tears are exhausted, there is always the same haunting, unanswered question: Where does human emotion end and adoration begin?

Lord,
when I am hungry, give me someone in
            need of food;
when I am thirsty, send me someone needing
            a drink;
when I am cold, send me someone to warm;
when I am grieved, offer me someone to
            console;
when my cross grows heavy, let me share
            another's cross too;
when I am poor, lead me to someone in
            need;
when I have no time, give me someone I
            can help a little while;
when I am humiliated, let me have
            someone to praise;
when I am disheartened, send me someone
            to cheer;
when I need people's understanding, give
            me someone who needs mine;
when I need to be looked after, send me
            someone to care for;
when I think only of myself, draw my
            thoughts to another.

                                    from a Japanese Co-worker

THE LINK FOR THE SICK AND SUFFERING

Inquiries relating to the Link for the Sick and Suffering should be addressed to:

The International Link for Sick and Suffering Co-workers,
Karel Oomstraat 14,
2000 Antwerp,
Belgium.